HOW TO WRITE ESSAYS

HOW TO WRITE ESSAYS

Roger Lewis

NATIONAL
EXTENSION
COLLEGE

Collins Educational

An imprint of HarperCollins*Publishers*

Published by
Collins Educational Ltd
77-85 Fulham Palace Road
Hammersmith
London W6 8JB

First published in 1993
Reprinted 1994
Reprinted 1995 (twice), 1996, 1997

The National Extension College (NEC) is an educational trust with a distinguished body of trustees. Since it was established in 1963, it has pioneered the development of flexible learning for adults. NEC is actively developing innovative materials and systems for distance learning on over 100 courses, from basic skills to degree and professional training. Working in partnership with Collins Educational, NEC can now offer the best in flexible learning materials to the widest possible audience and further its aim of extending educational opportunities for all.

About the author:

Roger Lewis has taught in primary and secondary schools, adult and higher education. He is currently the BP Professor of Learning Development at the University of Humberside. He has written many books for students and teachers. Roger has gained most of his own qualifications through independent study.

The publishers wish to thank Tim Burton for his invaluable editorial expertise.

British Library Cataloguing-in-Publication Data

A catalogue record for
this book is
available from the
British Library.

ISBN 0 00 327620 1

Typeset by Graham Hiles. Cover design by Information Design Workshop. Printed in Hong Kong.

Contents

Unit 1   **Introduction**   **7**
What level does the book aim at?   8
How do I use the book?   8
How is the book organised?   9
How long will it take?   9
Do I need any other books?   9

Unit 2   **Writing to learn and communicate**   **11**
Why essays seem difficult   11
Writing to learn   12
The differences between speaking and writing   12
A note on Units 3 to 11   15

Unit 3   **Analysing the question: key verbs and key ideas**   **19**
Answering the question   19
Key verbs   20
Key ideas   22
List of key verbs   24

Unit 4   **Brainstorming and probing**   **27**
Brainstorming   27
Probing   30

Unit 5   **Making notes**   **33**
The purpose of note-making   33
Using sources   34
Using your own words   35
Notes are personal   38

Unit 6   **Planning**   **43**
Planning in daily life   43
Planning an essay   44
How people plan essays   46
Choosing a planning method   49
Key verbs again   50

Unit 7   **Paragraphing**   **53**
The planning stage and writing paragraphs   53
What is a paragraph?   54
Signposting   60

Unit 8   **Drafting and checking**   **63**
Drafting   63

Unit 9   **Introductions and conclusions**   **69**
Introductions   69
Conclusions   70
How long should introductions and conclusions be?   71

Unit 10   **Getting your English right**   **73**
How to write clearly   73

Unit 11   **Presentation**   **79**
              Before writing the final copy   79
              Writing the finished copy   81
              After writing the finished copy   81

Unit 12   **Learning from comments**   **83**
              Marks   83
              Using the comments of others   86
              Conclusion   87

Appendix 1   Setting your own essay title   89

Appendix 2   Essays in examinations   91

Appendix 3   An essay writer's checklist   92

Appendix 4   Further reading   93

UNIT

1

INTRODUCTION

Writing essays scares many students. They have ideas, they can talk about their learning, but when it comes to putting words down on paper, for a tutor to read, they freeze up. Yet writing essays is a job like any other and in essence it is similar to many other tasks we carry out in our daily lives.

(This symbol indicates a Self-Assessment Question or SAQ. I'll explain SAQs later in this unit.)

Write down four activities you regularly carry out which require some kind of skill (e.g. making custard, checking the oil in the car). Read on only after you have written down your answer to this question.

I can't know what you wrote down but here are my answers:

■ tying a shoelace;

■ boiling an egg;

■ servicing a bicycle;

■ removing condensation from windows.

These are mainly small activities. But to carry them out successfully, I need:

■ knowledge;

■ a need or purpose;

■ skills;

■ a willingness to act, or the right attitude.

Let's take the example of servicing a bicycle. I need to:

■ know where to apply oil, and which components to check;

■ understand why I am carrying out the various tasks;

■ have manual skills, e.g. in adjusting brakes;

■ want to do it or at least to accept the importance of maintaining the bicycle.

1 Take one activity from the list you made. Break that activity down into knowledge, purpose, skill and attitude, as I have done for the bicycle.

It's interesting to see how wide-ranging the knowledge, purposes, skills and attitudes are in our everyday life, e.g. in running a home, getting to work, holding down a job or playing a sport. When we're used to doing something we tend to take for granted what's involved in doing it.

Essay writing, too, is a combination of knowledge, purpose, skill and attitude. We need to:

- have something to say (knowledge);
- have a reason for saying it to someone (purpose);
- be able to express ourselves in writing (skill);
- want to tackle the job (attitude).

Unfortunately it's the last one listed – a willing attitude – that many students lack. Writing essays seems a puzzling and lonely activity, much more difficult than other things in life. The criticism we have experienced (at school, for example) may well have undermined our confidence and our willingness to try.

This book relates essay writing to other activities, to build up your confidence and to show that the qualities required are not particularly unusual. It also offers guidance on how to collect and organise knowledge and how to write it up. Writing an essay is broken into four stages:

1   pre-writing;

2   planning;

3   drafting;

4   editing.

These are described more fully in the next unit. Considering these stages separately will help you to reflect on your own essay writing and that, in the end, is what will help you to improve it. The rest of this introduction answers questions which you may have about this book.

What level does the book aim at?

I have tried to write this book so that it will help students whatever their subject and whatever level they are studying. I have used as wide a range of essay topics as I could, to appeal to students taking a variety of subjects. The qualities (skills and understanding) needed to write essays apply equally across levels and across subjects. You will find, though, that you will have to adapt what is said to suit your own circumstances. Please note that I assume you can write English with reasonable fluency.

If you feel you need extra help with your writing, the books listed in Appendix 4, 'Further reading', may be helpful.

This book will also be of use to those who need to write reports, papers or other kinds of written work. I concentrate on essays, but the same skills are needed for organising all kinds of written work.

For more specific help on report writing see the NEC publication *Report Writing*: information on obtaining this is provided in Appendix 4, 'Further reading'.

How do I use the book?

You may be studying in one of the following ways:

- You may have bought the book from a bookshop and plan to work through it on your own.
- You may be a student at college, who has been advised by a tutor to look at certain parts of this book.

Ideally you will also be taking a course, one which requires you to write essays. That way you can try out some of the ideas in this book in your real-life studying.

How is the book organised?

It is important to understand some of the ways in which the book is put together, so you can use it to the full. This is not a textbook; it is a book designed to help you to learn for yourself. So I have included a number of special features.

Self-Assessment Questions (SAQs)

SAQs are always indicated by this symbol. When you see this symbol, stop, read over the question, and then write down your own answer. Only when you have answered the question for yourself should you go on to see how I have answered it. Some SAQs will have 'right' answers. But most are matters of emphasis and various answers are possible, so you should not worry if you disagree slightly with me. Please remember this; don't expect your answers to be exactly the same as mine. Use a sheet of A4 paper to stop yourself reading the answer before you have written down your own.

SAQs are your chance to check your understanding of what I've written and to practise the ideas in the book. The questions will make you think and write. Remember that both thinking and writing are essential parts of the writing process, whether you are working on an essay or on some other form of written communication.

What this unit is about

Each of the subsequent units in this book (from Unit 2 to Unit 12) begins with this heading. In 'What this unit is about' you'll find an outline of what the unit contains. You can judge from the outline whether or not you need to work through the unit. This book on essay writing is planned for flexible use: you can study the units in the order you find most useful and you can miss out units if you wish.

Check your learning

You will find this section at the end of each unit. It gives you the chance to review your progress and to find out how much you have learned as a result of your work on the unit.

Treat the SAQs and 'Check your learning' as further steps to learning rather than as obstacles to be overcome. Don't worry about making mistakes; the word error originally meant 'wandering about looking for something'. It is through making errors that we learn things, and find what it is we are looking for.

How long will it take?

If you are dipping into the book, then clearly it takes as long as you choose to spend on it. If you are working through it systematically, then it will take about three or four months. But students vary greatly in how long they spend.

Do I need any other books?

This book is self-contained but you should have at your side a good, modern dictionary. (Some suitable ones are listed in Appendix 4.) You should use your dictionary to check the spelling and meanings of any new words you meet. If you are studying a subject alongside this book (e.g. psychology, history) it would also be a good idea to keep your own notebook, listing important words and terms for the subject together with their meanings.

Check your learning

Page 9 explains the purpose of the 'Check your learning' sections. Write down the answers to the questions which follow. Do not look ahead to my answers until you have written down your own. Cover up the answer section with a sheet of A4 paper.

1 According to this introduction which of the following statements is correct?

    a   This book applies only to essays.

    b   This book can easily be adapted to other kinds of written work such as projects and reports.

2 According to this book which of the following statements is correct?

    a   Essay writing is related to other activities we carry out in daily life.

    b   Essay writing requires mysterious skills which we do not use in ordinary life.

3 Write notes (a few words for each) on how each of the following may help you to learn:

    a   a dictionary;

    b   the SAQs and 'Check your learning' in this book;

    c   the 'What this unit is about' sections in this book.

Read on only when you have answered the questions yourself.

Answers

1 Statement (b) is right. (See page 8.)

2 Statement (a) is right. (See pages 7–8.)

3 a   A dictionary helps you to check on the spellings and meanings of words.

    b   These help you to check your own progress and understanding – in the case of the SAQs, as you go through each unit; in the case of 'Check your learning', at the end of each unit.

    c   By looking at the 'What this unit is about' section you can find out what each unit covers. You can then decide whether or not you need to study that unit.

UNIT 2

WRITING TO LEARN AND COMMUNICATE

What this unit is about

This unit explains the purposes behind writing essays and is a foundation for the more detailed units that follow.

By the time you have finished your work on this unit, you should be able to:

→ explain how writing essays helps us to learn;

→ list some differences between communicating by speaking and communicating by writing;

→ state four stages that together give a framework for writing an essay.

Why essays seem difficult

It may be useful to consider how and why we write. Some kinds of writing seem as natural and effortless as speaking – for example, a letter to a close friend, or instructions for a task we know well. But for most of us, there is nothing natural or effortless about writing essays.

1 Can you suggest some reasons why essays seem more difficult than other kinds of writing? (Don't forget to use your A4 sheet to cover up my response.)

I can think of three reasons. (You may have thought of others.) First, essays tend to be about subjects that we don't know very well; we have no personal experience to draw from. In fact, we are writing the essay in order to learn. (We shall see later how important this is.) Second, essay questions are often deliberately phrased in a difficult way, so that the students are forced to think carefully about what the question means. You have to ask yourself what information your reader is interested in knowing, how much detail is appropriate, how to organise your essay.

Third, when we write an essay we may not know our reader very well. The reader may, indeed, be an examiner whom we will never meet. Thus we lack the confidence which comes from knowing well the person to whom we are writing.

Writing to learn

Perhaps the most important justification for writing an essay is that it helps us to learn – a point I made in my answer to SAQ 1. The verb 'to essay' means 'to put to the test, to attempt something difficult'. As students, we are, by definition, trying to learn to do something that is at present beyond us. We are putting ourselves to the test, and the essays we write give us the opportunity to measure how well we are doing; they are the means by which we learn. Essays give us the chance to come to terms with new knowledge. As we prepare the material for our essays, we are being forced to organise our thoughts clearly and to communicate them to a distant reader. We might think we grasp a subject, but writing an essay will force us to measure just how much we really understand. Essay writing tests a very wide range of skill and knowledge – e.g. the exact formulation of difficult concepts, and the ability to convey a complex logical argument. Here is an Open University student explaining how she has learned from writing essays:

> I find the essays actually crystallise ideas a lot. I read... and I end up with lots of what are essentially jumbled thoughts; I am not saying they don't make sense but there is no actual structure to them. You can see that one person says this and one person says that but the way in which these different ideas relate to each other... comes clear when I start writing.

Rarely does an essay come out right first time. We learn while writing and rewriting it, and afterwards from the comments of our readers or tutors.

Of course, we also learn by speaking. We may 'talk something over' with a friend. Often we understand our own minds more clearly after putting our thoughts or feelings into words for someone else. We also use silent speech – we 'think things through for ourselves' and even (when no one is listening) talk to ourselves. (I find I do this when following instructions, for example when mixing weedkiller.)

 Can you think of a time during the past week when you have talked over some problem with a friend, member of your family or a colleague?

We often learn quite complex things through talking. We can learn from writing too, as the quote from the Open University student describes so well. But moving from speaking to writing makes new demands, even if the audience remains the same.

The differences between speaking and writing

To make sure that you understand the implications of this important point, I want you to read carefully the following two accounts. The first is an attempt to write down a conversation between two people (with some detail of how the individuals look and move), and the second is an extract from a letter.

The conversation

Passer by: 'scuse me *(hesitant delivery)*

Me: uhh yes *(turning round)*

Passer by: *(making eye contact)* could you direct me to the post office *(pitch of voice rises at end of sentence)*

Me: *(confused at first, playing for time)* oh hang on a minute go up there *(looks and points up the road)*

Passer by: sorry up there *(pitch of voice rises; raises eyebrows and looks in the same direction)*

Me: mmm *(eyes meet)* carry on up a few hundred yards. It's up a turning on *(looks down)* wait a minute *(waves left hand)* on this side *(emphasises 'this')*

The letter

> With 92 Stockton Lane on your right, go up the road, leaving the town behind you. Go past the first turning on your right until you reach a private hotel standing on the corner of a turning. Turn right there, and you will find the Post Office about one hundred yards down on your left.

 Compare the conversation and the letter. What are the main differences between them? (As always, please cover up the response that follows, until you have finished writing your own answer.)

You may have written something like this:

- written: seems more to the point;
- spoken: seems rambling;
- spoken: more attention to people's looks, movements and feelings;
- written: more formal and uses punctuation (commas, full stops);
- spoken: uses gestures, pauses.

When two people are talking they have more than just the words to help convey their meaning.

 What other things besides words convey meaning in a conversation?

Gesture and facial expression are two very important aids. Hence in my example, there was a fair bit of pointing and turning – physical acts which are useless when you are trying to explain things to someone on paper. Then again, the speaker can notice expressions on the listener's face. A raised eyebrow, frown or look of uncertainty can show the need to repeat something, put it in a different way, add to it or shorten it. In the case of a conversation, the communication is two-way; the listener can ask for more information and there's a good deal of social talk and expression of feeling. It's possible, too, to convey much meaning by the words we choose to emphasise.

From the conversation on the previous page, write down one example of each of the following:
- a a gesture;
- b facial expression;
- c the passer by asking for more help;
- d social contact;
- e emphasis on particular words.

Here are my ideas:

a   points up road; waves left hand;

b   raises eyebrows;

c   'sorry up there';

d   ''scuse me';

e   'on this side' – emphasises 'this'.

(You may have noted down other examples.)

In a written communication nearly all these aids are either lacking or have to be created by different means. Gestures, spoken emphasis, expressions on the face – all these are impossible. Your reader cannot easily ask you to clear up something they haven't understood. The separation of writer and reader means that you have to communicate on paper only – the written marks are all that your audience has to go on.

The written word thus makes considerable demands on us as writers. We must:

- ■ choose words with great care;

- ■ place them in the best order;

- ■ make sure the structure of our points is clear and logical;

- ■ anticipate our readers' needs;

- ■ punctuate and spell very carefully.

Words are all a reader has to go on. When you write an essay your meaning must be there on the page, clear. Your reader cannot always ask you to explain muddled passages.

Nonetheless, writing does have advantages over speech.

What are the advantages of written communication?

The written word preserves thoughts and feelings; other people can come along and read these and we ourselves can rework them. Some people prefer to write because they can consider more fully what they want to say; they do not have to commit themselves on the spot, as when speaking. It's possible to make several attempts (or 'drafts') of a written communication until it's right. Written words also have advantages for the reader who can turn to them at any time. Just as writers can take time and consider, so too can readers. They can choose their own reading pace; they can look ahead and look back over what they are reading; they can return to what has been written, think about it, check it.

A note on Units 3 to 11

So far, we have looked at how writing is different from spoken communication; we have also considered how essays are different from other forms of writing. In the following units (Units 3 to 11), we will be looking step by step at the various stages in writing an essay. You may be beginning to feel that writing an essay is an overwhelmingly complex task. It is true that there are many factors to keep in mind:

1   What is the purpose or requirement of the essay assignment?

2   What do you know about the subject?

3   Which aspects of the subject do you need to think through more fully?

4   Is there additional information you need?

✱5   How detailed should you be in developing and supporting your ideas?

6   What is appropriate? Interesting? Important?

7   How can you organise your essay effectively?

8   Who is your reader? How can you best convey your ideas to this reader?

9   What difficulties might the reader encounter?

10   How should you introduce and conclude the essay?

11   When should you proofread for spelling, punctuation, paragraph and sentence structure?

While these are all significant concerns, trying to attend to several at once or in a random manner leads only to confusion. However, the complexities become manageable if you approach essay writing in stages. The units that follow are arranged to assist you as you write essays.

Stage 1 Pre-writing

In this initial stage, the writer tries to understand what the essay requires, notes existing knowledge and also what information has still to be collected. Pre-writing is discussed in these units:

Unit 3: *Analysing the question: key verbs and key ideas*

Unit 4: *Brainstorming and probing*

Unit 5: *Taking notes*

Stage 2 Planning

The writer summarises, organises and rearranges the notes taken at the pre-writing stage, looking for connections and directions. Planning is discussed in these units:

Unit 6: *Planning*

Unit 7: *Paragraphing*

Stage 3 Drafting

The writer shapes the notes into an essay. At the drafting stage, the writer returns repeatedly to the pre-writing and planning stages. Gradually, by rethinking and rewriting the draft, the writer develops a point of view. Drafting is discussed in these units:

Unit 8: *Drafting and checking*

Unit 9: *Introductions and conclusions*

Stage 4 Editing

Once the essay is written, it is carefully proofread to eliminate any errors in spelling or punctuation. At this final stage, the writer also rewrites any clumsy or unclear sentences. Editing is discussed in these units:

Unit 10: *Getting your English right*

Unit 11: *Presentation*

Check your learning

1   Which of the following statements is the 'odd one out'?

In speaking to one another we often:

a   use facial expression;

b   use gesture;

c   use the other person's responses to help decide what to say next;

d   use words and phrases to help maintain social contact;

e   talk non-stop.

2   Draw up two columns, one headed 'Speaking' and the other headed 'Writing'. List two differences between these forms of communication.

3   List two demands writing makes on the writer.

4   Give one advantage writing has over speaking.

5   What are the four main stages of essay writing?

Read on only when you have answered the questions yourself. Use your A4 sheet to cover up my answer until you are ready.

Answers

1   Statement (e) is the odd one out. Most of us don't!

2

Speaking	Writing
Used often to establish and maintain personal relationships.	Often used for more formal purposes.
'Audience' is present, specific, and often known personally to the speaker.	'Audience' distant.
'Audience' gives an immediate reply.	Delayed reply or no reply at all.
There are repetitions, pauses, gaps, etc.; all these help the listener to make sense of the message.	Writing uses words tightly and sequentially; other devices (e.g. punctuation) help meaning.
Speech cannot (except with a tape recorder) be replayed; it fades.	Writing is permanent; it can be read many times over.
Tends to use more words.	Tends to be condensed.
Body, expression, movement are often important in conveying meaning.	All the meaning is in the words.

(You may have put these points differently or found other good points of your own. You were asked for only two differences.)

3   Careful choice of words

Attention to structure of points

Careful spelling and punctuation.

(See the text for other possible answers.)

4   Writers can consider what they want to say. Readers can check back, pause, choose their own reading speed.

(See the text for other possible answers.)

5   Pre-writing, planning, drafting and editing.

ANALYSING THE QUESTION

KEY VERBS AND KEY IDEAS

What this unit is about

This is the first of three units which cover the pre-writing stage. By the time you have finished your work on this unit, you should be able to:

→ pick out the key verbs and key ideas in an essay question;

→ analyse the question-setter's intent in setting the question.

Answering the question

If we ask someone a question in daily life we expect it to be answered. If we ask how to replace a spark plug we do not want to be told how spark plugs are manufactured; if we ask how much washing up liquid costs then we should be puzzled if we were told only what its ingredients are.

In most courses specific essay questions are set. These questions have been carefully phrased to tell you exactly what to do with a given topic. Yet time and again students ignore the help given in the question and so lose marks. (If you have to set your own essay titles then see Appendix 1 as well as working through this unit.)

Analysing the question helps you to think about what the person who set the question has in mind, to locate the purpose behind it. Is a description wanted? A narrative? An argument? An explanation? Is the treatment to be factual? Imaginative?

1 Read the following two essay questions. Write a sentence or two on the purpose that lies behind each question. What kind of writing do you think is required?
a   Describe a time when you were afraid.
b   Assess the main causes of the First World War.

The first essay question asks for personal experience. The second wants an historical analysis. (Before we could be absolutely sure, we would need to know more about the course from which each essay question was taken.)

2 Read the openings of answers to the two essay questions on the next page. Do these openings seem to you to be answering the question? Has each student interpreted correctly what the question requires?

(continued overleaf)

> Describe a time when you were afraid.
>
> *Fear has meant many things at different times. Once people feared wild animals; then they feared man-made objects, like aeroplanes. In the nineteenth century, they feared revolution and famine.*

> Assess the main causes of the First World War.
>
> *Bodies lay pell-mell, some torn by barbed wire, some resting sadly in mud and puddles. Smoke drifted above the battlefield. No-man's land assumed an uneasy quiet.*

Neither opening seems to be right. The opening to the first essay is too general and semi-factual. The second opening shows the opposite failing: too great an emphasis on the 'creative' and imaginative. The second essay requires the writer to stand back and look at causes, not events or results, or anyone's specific experiences. A good opening sentence for this essay question might be:

> *Of the many possible causes of the First World War, the rise of nationalism seems the most important.*

The rest of this unit helps you to tackle systematically the task of uncovering the key verbs and key ideas in essay questions.

Key verbs

Clearly it is important to work out the content (or subject matter) of a question, but this is usually straightforward. What you need to look at more closely are the words which indicate how you are expected to discuss this content – the key verbs which tell you what treatment you are expected to give this content.

It is not only in writing essays that we have to attend to key verbs which tell us what to do. Our behaviour on the roads is directed all the time by signs – 'No Left Turn', 'Pass Either Side', 'Slow Down'. In public buildings (such as swimming pools) we are told 'Enter here', 'Take an armband', 'Take your key with you'.

3 Underline the verbs (and any other words) which tell you how to behave, or which give you directions, in the following:
a Apply the paste thinly.
b Plant the shoots at intervals of 3 inches.
c Mix the powder with a little water.
d Use blank cartridges.

Use your A4 sheet to cover the response!

Strictly speaking the verbs are apply, plant, mix and use. You would not have been wrong though if you had picked out a few other words which explain the verb a little more fully, e.g.

Apply the paste *thinly*.

Plant the shoots *at intervals of 3 inches*.

Mix the powder *with a little water*.

Notice that 'paste', 'shoots', 'powder' and 'cartridges' give the subject matter. The italicised words tell you what to do with the things, how to treat them. They give you essential information as to how you should carry out the necessary task. You would be a fool if you ignored them: you would waste money, or time, or even endanger life. Yet students very frequently ignore the key verbs in their essay titles.

4 You were asked earlier to look at this question: 'Assess the main causes of the First World War.' Now – underline the key verb in it.

The verb is 'assess' (it's the only verb in the question). It tells you how you are expected to write about the causes. Another significant little word is 'main'. You are not expected to write about every possible cause, only the main ones.

5 Underline the key verb in each of the following questions. Remember: the key verb tells you how to proceed.
  a Narrate the main events of Gladstone's second ministry.
  b Explain the principal causes of the French Revolution.
  c Describe how a glacier is formed.
  d Tell us what happened to you on your way to the exam room.

'Narrate', 'explain', 'describe' and 'tell' are the key verbs. Notice also how 'main' and 'principal' come into the first two questions.

Sorting out the key verb sets you on the right path. You are not asked to write generally about the above topics (the second ministry, glaciers, etc.) but to cover particular aspects in a particular way. The following SAQ gives you more practice.

6 Read the following essay questions and answer the questions which follow.
  a 'Society today is totally different from society in 1900.' Justify this statement.
  b 'Society today is totally different from society in 1900.' Outline the main stages of change between 1900 and today.
  c 'Society today is totally different from society in 1900.' Evaluate this statement.
  d 'Society today is totally different from society in 1900.' Diagnose the main causes of change.

  1 What is the subject matter of the four questions?

  2 Underline the words which show how in each case the student must treat the subject matter in a particular way.

1 The subject matter is the same for each question and is given in the first sentence (which, as often in essay titles, is a quotation): the contrast between society in 1900 and society today.

2 The second sentence indicates how the student should handle the subject matter. In each case the student is asked to do something different:

a *Justify* the statement;

b *Outline* the main stages of change;

c *Evaluate* this statement;

d *Diagnose* the main causes of change.

Notice that it's the main *stages* of change the student is to deal with in (b) and the main *causes* of change in (d).

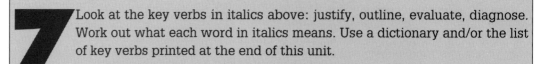

Look at the key verbs in italics above: justify, outline, evaluate, diagnose. Work out what each word in italics means. Use a dictionary and/or the list of key verbs printed at the end of this unit.

It's well worth spending time exploring the meanings of such words – you should get into the habit of using a dictionary for this.

The first three words are also in the list of key verbs at the end of this unit. 'Diagnose' means 'work out' (or similar).

The essay questions on which we have just been working lead us to the second part of this unit: identifying the key ideas in an essay title.

Key ideas

Often an essay question will contain within it not just the key verb but also a key idea. In the example we looked at in SAQ 6 we have the idea 'society'; the word seems self-evident but in social science the student must learn how to define 'society' and how to analyse its component parts. Another example from social science is the phrase 'middle class' as in the question

'We are all middle class now.' Discuss.

It isn't possible to answer this without a clear idea of what 'middle class' means. Is it to do with income, education, speech, profession, life style – or particular combinations of these? The answer to the question will depend on the way the term is defined; this will have to be explained in each individual student's answer.

The ideas that matter for you will depend on your own subject and on the level of your course.

If you are studying another course at the same time as this book, then write down three key ideas that frequently occur in your studies. Here is an example:

Geography – contour, region, climate.

9 Underline the key verbs and the key ideas in each of the following essay questions:
   a 'The aim of education is personal fulfilment.' Discuss.
   b 'Absence of discipline is the cause of the problems in today's schools.' Evaluate this view.

Key verbs		Key ideas
a	discuss	education, personal fulfilment
b	evaluate	discipline

Taken together, key verbs and key ideas help you to limit your treatment of the subject matter in the way the question requires. They help you to mark out the area you are going to cover. If you make this kind of careful analysis of your question then you are much more likely to collect material that is relevant. A history tutor has provided two very good examples of how students can waste their time and energy by failing to look closely enough at the question:

> In Worksheet A, a question asks students to decide whether 'expediency' or 'policy' motivated reforms before 1830. Many students write an account of reforms but never use the words 'expediency' or 'policy' at all.
>
> In Worksheet C we have the question 'What was the long-term significance of the chief measures of reform relating to England during Gladstone's First Ministry?' About half my students begin with reforms relating to Ireland. All the essays give detailed descriptions of the reforms. Not one has ever posed the question 'What is demanded by the expression "long term significance?"' And I have marked hundreds!

Picking out key verbs and ideas is one way to analyse an essay question. But sometimes there is no key verb or key idea; they are only implied, not directly stated. Then the job of analysing the question becomes more complex. SAQ 10 gives you practice in looking for key verbs and key ideas hidden or implied in the question.

10 The following questions are taken from a technology course. The topic is CHP or combined heat and power schemes. (CHP schemes convert power stations to produce hot water as well as electricity.) You do not need to know anything about CHP to answer them.

Read each question carefully and write, in a sentence or two, the intention of the person setting the question. If the key verb is not directly stated, say what you think it might be. (The list of key verbs at the end of this unit is a useful reference.)

   a What are the main advantages of CHP schemes?
   b What implications do CHP schemes have for the electricity industry?
   c In anticipation of the 'energy crisis' what new forms of energy production or supply need urgent consideration?
   d Choose one area in Britain and outline how you would convert existing stock to enable a CHP scheme to operate.
   e Can CHP schemes be justified economically in rural areas?

a   The key verb is not actually stated but the student is being asked to 'state', 'outline', 'explain', 'analyse' or 'evaluate'. Discussion of the disadvantages, or problems, of CHP schemes is not required. An answer may need to mention other schemes over which CHP schemes have advantages.

b   Again, no key verb is stated. The question seems to require the student to 'assess' or 'evaluate' the implications CHP schemes have for the electricity industry. (Notice the way 'electricity' narrows the question down; other industries need not be discussed.)

c   This question requires the student to 'state', 'explain' or 'outline' new forms of energy production. CHP might be one of these; in the particular technology course it is mentioned alongside wave power, wind power, and solar power. 'Energy crisis' seems a key idea; note that it is given status by being enclosed in quotation marks.

d   The student must choose (one area in Britain, not several areas, and only in Britain) and outline. . . This question is more technical than the others. It asks the student to show knowledge of how to convert machinery and plant so that a CHP scheme might operate.

e   A 'discuss' or 'explore' question which might have been written:

Consider (or discuss or explore) whether CHP schemes are justified economically in rural areas.

Notice the way this question is shaped by its key ideas – towards an economic treatment, and limited to schemes in rural areas.

SAQ 10 has dealt with more complex questions which don't give the student clear and direct key verbs. Be on the look-out for questions like these (you may or may not get them in your courses). You should, though, be able to use the work you have done earlier in this unit to establish what lies behind such questions.

Some of what I have said about analysing the question may seem very obvious. But again and again, all over the country and in every subject, able students fail to do themselves justice because they fail to answer the question. Looking at the question carefully is essential to laying the foundation of a sound answer. It only takes a few minutes, but those few minutes are vital to later success. I have suggested some simple procedures. They will need to be adapted to suit your subject and course. You may not always find clear key verbs or ideas in your essay question. You should now, however, be able to use a strategy for uncovering the intention behind the questions you have to answer. In many courses, you may be required to set your own title. For some advice on how to do this see Appendix 1, 'Setting your own essay title'.

List of key verbs

The following verbs appear frequently in essay questions. Make sure that you are quite clear about the meaning of each of them. Use this list to refer back to later in your studies.

Analyse	Break up into parts, investigate
Compare	Look for similarities and differences between; perhaps reach a conclusion about which is preferable
Contrast	Bring out differences between
Criticise	See *evaluate*
Define	Set down the meaning of a word or phrase
Delineate	See *outline*

Describe	Give a detailed account of
Differentiate	See *distinguish between*
Discuss	Investigate or examine by argument; sift and debate; give reasons for and against; also examine the implications
Distinguish between	Indicate the differences between
Enumerate	See *outline*
Evaluate	Give your judgement about the merit of theories or opinions; back your judgement by a discussion of evidence or reasoning involved
Examine	Look closely into
Explain	Make plain; interpret and account for; give reasons for
Explore	Examine thoroughly, consider from a variety of viewpoints
Illustrate	See *interpret*
Interpret	Make clear and explicit; show the meaning of
Justify	Show adequate grounds for decisions or conclusions; answer the main objections likely to be made to them
List	See *outline*
Outline	Give the main features or general principles of a subject, omitting minor details and emphasising structure and arrangement
Relate	a Narrate – more usual in examinations
	b Show how things are connected to each other, and to what extent they are alike, or affect each other
Review	See *summarise*
State	Present in a brief, clear form
Summarise	Give a concise account of the chief points of a matter, omitting details and examples
Trace	Follow the development or history of a topic from some point of origin.

Check your learning

1 Underline the key verbs (and any associated relevant words) in the following:

a Evaluate the success of Palmerston's foreign policy.

b Give an account of Palmerston's foreign policy.

c 'Palmerston's foreign policy was fundamentally unsound.' Discuss critically.

d How did Palmerston promote British interests?

e Why did Palmerston promote British interests?

2 What is the key idea in (d) and (e) of Question 1?

3 Find the key verbs and key ideas in each of the following. Use different coloured inks for verb and idea, or different kinds of underlining, or draw up a box like this:

Question	Verb	Idea
A		
B		

    a   Define 'capitalism' and list the features of Britain's political and economic system that could be called 'capitalist'.

    b   Evaluate the contributions made to British dress sense by one named person from each of the following categories:

- media personalities;

- sportsmen and women;

- politicians.

4   Consider the following responses to the two essay topics from Question 3:

    a   The student discusses the capitalist economies of the world.

    b   The student starts by defining 'dress sense'.

Are they adequate ways to respond to the essay questions? Comment on each response.

Read on only when you have answered the questions yourself.

Answers

1   a   Evaluate

    b   Give an account of...

    c   Discuss critically ('critically' expands the key verb)

    d   How did Palmerston promote...

    e   Why...

2   'British interests'

3

Question	Verb	Idea
A	define and list	capitalism; Britain's political and economic system; capitalist
B	evaluate	British dress sense

Note

In question (a) 'capitalism' (and 'capitalist') are clearly key concepts, but so is 'Britain's political and economic system'. A political and economic system could be said to include several key concepts.

4   a   This response looks in danger of being irrelevant. The question clearly asks for a discussion of *Britain's* economy from this point of view.

    b   Adequate. It is sensible to explain what you are taking a key idea to mean.

UNIT 4

BRAINSTORMING AND PROBING

What this unit is about

This unit introduces you to two pre-writing techniques: brainstorming and probing.

By the time you have finished your work on this unit, you should be able to:

→   define brainstorming and probing;

→   use brainstorming and probing techniques to collect ideas and information for an essay.

Brainstorming

1   Look up 'brainstorm' in your dictionary. Brace yourself for what you find.

The *Collins New Compact English Dictionary* I have in front of me gives several definitions for brainstorm, including the following: 'a sudden mental aberration'. Read on before you close the book in alarm.

However, the definition given for 'brainstorming' recognises how the meaning has grown in recent years to include intensive discussion to solve problems or generate ideas. Brainstorming is helpful because it shows you what you already know about a topic – either because it is a topic on which everyone will have ideas (as with the topic we turn to in a moment) or because you have studied the topic as part of a course. Before turning to books and notes you can discover that you already possess useful information. Students often neglect this activity but it takes only a short while and can help enormously, both in increasing your confidence and in helping you to see what shape your answer might take.

To brainstorm you should first clear away all your books and papers. You need just a blank sheet of paper and a pen. Look at the essay topic and write as many points as you can in, say, ten minutes. Don't worry at this stage if some of what you write seems wild or irrelevant. Most students are surprised at how much they can produce. Let's practise on one of the essay questions from the last unit.

'Society today is totally different from society in 1900.' Evaluate this statement.

In SAQ 6 of the last unit you examined this question. Now I'd like you to brainstorm. But first an important point: I've set you a very artificial task. In real life you would encounter this essay as part of a course and you would have collected facts and information from your reading. I am giving you this question entirely out of context. This reduces the value of the exercise. But I still hope that you will try it. I've chosen the question because I think most of you will be able to think of something to write.

2 Take a sheet of blank paper. Brainstorm for this essay title:

'Society today is totally different from society in 1900.' Evaluate this statement.

Figure 4.1 shows how one student recorded her ideas.

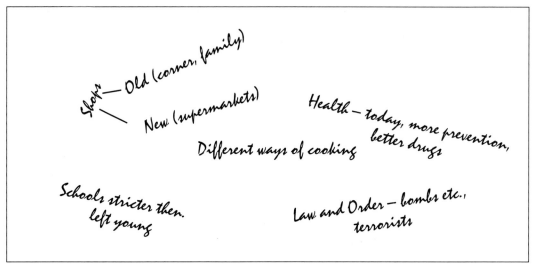

Shops — Old (corner, family)

New (supermarkets)

Different ways of cooking

Health — today, more prevention, better drugs

Schools stricter then. left young

Law and Order — bombs etc., terrorists

Figure 4.1 Response to SAQ 2

I've given you just enough to show you one way of doing it. The student writes points anywhere on the page, in spaces. They can be rearranged, sorted, classified later. But at the brainstorming stage all you try to do is to get them down in a way that works for you.

N.B. If you are using a word processor, you might like to try brainstorming on screen.

Another way is to write a list:

— *more marriage problems today*

— *working wives*

— *families split up — working away from home*

— *Less family care for the elderly*

A third way to record notes is to write the title in the centre of the page (in a shortened form), and then to write points off from the centre. This type of note-taking, called patterned notes, is shown in Figure 4.2. The main points are on the first stalk; examples branch out from the main stalk.

Experiment with various methods of recording brainstorming notes until you find one that suits you. The method isn't important. What is important is that you get down on paper the ideas and knowledge you already have. Some of what you record may not be particularly useful; not all of it will end up in the final essay. But your brainstorming notes will provide you with invaluable 'leads' to direct your further reading and thinking.

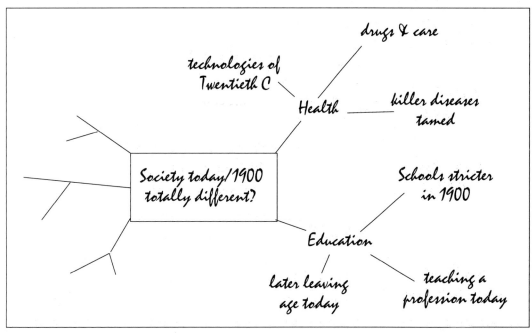

Figure 4.2 An example of patterned notes

Brainstorming should feel like a creative, enjoyable activity. Freed of all your books and notes, you experience yourself as a source of ideas. If you generally find it difficult to think of enough to write in essays, then almost certainly you need to work particularly hard at this stage. Brainstorming helps you to explore the topic and to uncover ideas which you can later play with and expand.

Probing

When you work on a new essay topic you will nearly always have to collect information from books, people, programmes and from other sources. You will not in most cases be able to answer the question straightaway. Brainstorming shows you what you know. Probing shows you what you need to find out. At the probing stage you simply write down the questions to which you'll seek answers. These questions are valuable in that they will guide your later research, the stage when you actually collect the material. Probing thus makes your later work more purposeful.

Let's look at an example. A student working on the question 'Society today is totally different from society in 1900' listed the following questions:

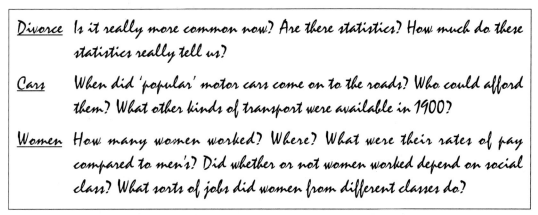

This gives you an idea of what's involved in probing. As with brainstorming, you can arrange your probing questions in any way – as lists, or in some patterned form.

3 Look back to your brainstormed notes taken in SAQ 2. Now practise probing for the same essay question. Write down the questions you think you would have to try to answer. Use any shape or pattern for these questions – lists or whatever.

Probing is particularly useful for exploring the key ideas in a question title. (If you're not sure about how to identify key ideas, refer back to Unit 3.) The key idea in the essay title above might be probed as follows:

> *What is meant by 'society'? Customs? institutions (such as schools, churches)? politics? housing and material things? All of these?*

You could of course go much further, and ask questions about your questions, or work out possible answers before you turn to your books. If this were a real essay (for a course you were actually studying), your questions would be more specific because you would already have particular knowledge of the subject. The important thing to remember is this: don't just plunge into a pile of reading. Many students start to read and take notes straightaway from their books. But this can be an escape from thinking. Thinking about the question is essential to lay the basis for a sound and interesting answer.

Don't be afraid of stating or asking the obvious at the pre-writing stage. Your brainstorming and probing notes are only for your own use; no one else is going to see them. Later, as you plan and draft, you can modify your questions or delete information that isn't useful.

Brainstorming and probing don't have to take a lot of time; even half an hour on these pre-writing techniques would be time well spent. Your notes and questions will guide your reading and, in the long run, they will cut down on the amount of time you spend planning and drafting your essay.

Check your learning

1 Give two reasons for brainstorming.

2 The questions below are from different subjects. You probably think that you know little about most of them. Nevertheless, spend two or three minutes probing each topic, making up a few questions to which you would hope to find answers.

    a   Examine the problems of living in an area of volcanic activity.

    b   What steps did Gladstone take in his 'mission to pacify Ireland'?

    c   What are the functions of 'attitudes' for the individual?

Read on only when you have answered the questions yourself.

Answers

1   There are several reasons you might have mentioned:

- It helps you organise your answer to the essay.

- It gives you confidence.

- It uncovers useful material for the essay.

- It guides your later work on books and notes.

- It takes little time.

- It is a bridge from the known to the unknown.

2   Here are one or two examples of questions for each title:

a   What is volcanic activity? What area – where? What kind of problems? How far from volcano? What kind of living: physical safety? growing crops? working?

b   How many steps? Why did he want to 'pacify' Ireland? Why was Ireland angry? Was it all of Ireland, or only parts? What sort of measures did Gladstone take: physical force? acts of parliament? discussion with Irish leaders? economic aid?

c   How is 'attitude' being used here? What are some examples of attitudes? Do I have attitudes? If so, what functions do they serve for me? Is 'functions' being used in a particular way in this question?

UNIT 5

MAKING NOTES

What this unit is about

Unit 5, the last unit on pre-writing, will help you to develop your skills in note-making.

By the time you have finished your work on this unit, you should be able to:

➜   list the purposes notes may serve;

➜   link note-making to probing and brainstorming;

➜   state several sources of notes;

➜   explain why it is necessary to give details of sources;

➜   explain how to record sources;

➜   explain why notes should be in your own words;

➜   explore a variety of ways of making notes, and find one that works well for you.

The purpose of note-making

Making notes has consumed hours and hours of my time as a student. Sadly, most of those hours have been wasted. I keep coming across piles of notes which I hoped would 'come in useful one day'; but they never have. The truth is that for me, as for so many students, making notes only *seems* productive; too often it is a substitute for thinking. Before you make notes, think of the purpose they will serve.

1 From the book so far, and from your own experience, list some of the purposes notes can serve.

You may have listed such things as:

■   to keep our attention (on a book, a lecture, a programme); to record a reference to follow up later; to have material for revision;

■   to reconstruct, later, the content of a book or lecture;

■   to explain material to ourselves.

In this book we are concerned with a more particular reason for making notes: making notes to write an essay. Already you have seen note-making in action:

■   to help to analyse the question set (Unit 3);

- to brainstorm, i.e. to record our own existing knowledge (Unit 4);
- to probe, i.e. to ask questions to guide our work on books, articles, etc. (Unit 4);
- to work towards a fuller understanding of key ideas (Unit 4).

In this unit we shall look at notes made:

- to expand and improve on notes made while brainstorming;
- to answer the questions made at the probing stage;
- to record the information collected from sources of knowledge.

Using sources

After brainstorming and probing the essay topic, you should have a set of notes that:

- outlines the framework of what you already know;
- lists a series of questions to guide your further research.

You now turn to sources that will help you to:

- fill out the framework of knowledge you already have;
- answer your questions.

As you collect information from your sources, you will find yourself asking new questions, and thus modifying your earlier work.

At this stage, you must be careful to collect information that will really be useful. Some students don't collect enough information; others fall into the opposite trap and collect too much. Only experience helps you to strike the right balance.

How to find suitable sources

Each essay topic will lead you to some sources rather than others. If, for example, you are writing on the ways in which your community has changed over the past fifty years, then an important source would probably be people who have lived in your community over that period. In other words, interviews would be a way of carrying out the purposes just described – answering questions and expanding your knowledge.

Your source may be primarily yourself. If, for example, you are working on the topic of disciplining children, then what is primarily wanted is your own ideas. You would thus be trying to accumulate more knowledge about what you think on the topic. You might also, in the process of doing this, use other sources to help you to clarify your ideas. You might, for example, read books, talk to friends who have children or listen to a relevant radio programme.

Many topics will require you to seek out books and other printed sources (such as journal articles, encyclopedia entries, textbooks).

If you are writing about a topic of current interest (e.g. an international crisis) then newspaper and television/radio reports will be vital. It is important to be aware that a whole range of sources may be helpful to you. They won't all be books.

How to deal with the sources you find

I suggest a two-stage process: first a quick encounter, and then detailed study. You want to find out whether the source is relevant; if it is, then you need to spend time with it. For example, you might chat to various neighbours, but only interview one or two in detail. If you get several books from the library, you will use your probing questions to decide what you need from each one. The index and contents pages in the book will direct you to the relevant sections.

Recording your sources

Your reader may want to check on the sources you have used (e.g. to find out more about the topic, to assess the value of the source, to see how well you have used the source). They cannot do this unless you record the details of your sources and put these at the end of the essay. There's nothing mysterious about this. We do it every day:

> A *They're moving into that old house up the street.*
>
> B *Oh really? Who is?*
>
> A *New people from Yorkshire.*
>
> B *How do you know?*
>
> A *Jill Stevens told me.*

B can now estimate how reliable the information is – e.g. is Jill Stevens usually right? Would someone else be a better source? How can the information be double-checked?

If you are the source of a particular idea, then you don't need to say so; your reader will assume it. If, however, your sources are printed materials, such as books or journals, then you must identify them clearly. Usually, information on sources is presented in an alphabetical listing at the end of an essay. At the note-making stage, you must be sure to keep an accurate record of all your sources, so that you can easily retrieve this information when you prepare your final copy.

For information on how to acknowledge sources in the final copy of your essay, see Unit 11, 'Presentation'.

Using your own words

I began this chapter by describing a common form of wasting time: copying out what is in piles of books or articles. This only seems productive; our fingers are busy but not our brains. To put ideas into our own words is much more likely to guarantee understanding. Ideas put in our own words are ideas we have made our own. Let's take an example from the topic we have been following through – changes in society from 1900 to today.

Let's assume a student – Jim – is working on this essay question and in his reading he keeps coming across the phrase 'socio-cultural factors'. He has the choice of copying this phrase out, without really understanding it, or of trying to master it.

The first alternative is tempting but Jim is a conscientious student and he knows that in the end the second solution is better, although it will seem to slow up his reading.

Jim starts by trying to develop his understanding. He splits up the phrase into three. 'Factors' is easy, it means nothing much more than 'things'. 'Socio' is close to 'social' – 'people living together in a society'. 'Cultural' is tricky. 'Culture' is 'great art and music etc.' but that doesn't seem to fit. Jim then turns to some sentences in which the phrase is used and to a dictionary. He comes up as a result with this definition (his own, but based on his reading): 'A society's values and traditions'. But it seems a bit too general. What values and traditions? He lists some examples:

> *respect for monarchy*
>
> *formal weddings*
>
> *initiation into manhood*
>
> *ritual sacrifice*
>
> *Ascot*
>
> *opening of Parliament*
>
> *ritual bathing – Ganges*
>
> *Chinese New Year*

He thinks of other societies – primitive tribes, Britain in other periods of history, countries in the former Soviet Union – to help him to produce these examples.

Jim then produces three definitions of 'socio-cultural factors'. He tries to imagine a friend who knows nothing about the topic but who wants to know what the phrase means – this makes Jim work hard on the clarity of his definitions.

> *1   People develop their own set of customs, habits and procedures in order to live together. The choices they make show their values as a society.*
>
> *2   Basically different ways of life according to different cultures, customs or traditions of different sets of people all over the world. It's reflected in the way they live together.*
>
> *3   People are influenced by others in the groups in which they live. They prefer to continue to live in the manner to which they are accustomed, and which is accepted by those around them.*

Like many academic or technical terms, 'socio-cultural factors' is a bit of professional shorthand that compresses a great deal of meaning into a single phrase. The term needs to be explored and its precise meaning spelled out. Jim finally settles on the first and last definitions as best. His notes have helped him to understand the meaning of the idea. His time has been well spent because every time the phrase comes up in his work during the rest of the course he will feel confident that he understands it. It is often necessary to take passages from articles and textbooks and unravel them, confirming to yourself that you understand them by rephrasing the ideas in your own words – and checking your definition by imagining yourself putting it to a friend or a member of the family.

Notice the sequence that Jim follows:

- He realises he has a problem with a particular phrase.
- He splits the phrase up and has a go at writing down what it means.
- He looks at the sentence in which it is used.
- He uses a dictionary.
- He comes up with a definition, better than his first one but still not quite right.
- So he thinks up some relevant examples.
- He tries some more definitions, imagining a friend who is asking him to explain the difficult idea.
- He chooses the best definition.

2 Using any or all of Jim's strategies, try to make sense of this sample passage. Then answer the questions which follow.

Working class people have not created family and neighbourhood patterns of living suitable for high achievement on the part of their children in knowledge, in interpersonal skills, in aesthetic awareness, in understanding and in life generally. The working class serves the purpose of producing adequately capable labour power, not a flood of able, ambitious individualists with wide social horizons who desire to compete with those born into the higher strata.

(Source: Miliband, R *The State in Capitalist Society*, Quartet Books Limited 1973)

    a   What does this mean? (In your own words.)

    b   What do you think the following phrases mean?

       ■ 'interpersonal skills';

       ■ 'aesthetic awareness';

       ■ 'adequately capable labour power';

       ■ 'ambitious individualists';

       ■ 'higher strata'.

Use the A4 sheet to cover up my answers until you have written your own.

a   Working class parents do not bring their children up to succeed academically nor do they expect them to get 'good' jobs.

b   'interpersonal skills' – getting on with people

      'aesthetic awareness' – interest in art

      'adequately capable labour power' – reasonably good workers

      'ambitious individualists' – people keen to get on as individuals

      'higher strata' – higher social classes

These are the notes which I made on the passage, but you may well have arrived at a different understanding of this very complex piece of prose. Compare your notes with mine. Remember that the purpose of this SAQ is not for you to arrive at any 'right' answer, but for you to gain experience in unravelling a complex argument, and in defining key ideas. (Sometimes such passages are unnecessarily difficult and could have been more simply put. I don't want to enter that debate here: unfortunately a lot of 'academic' writing is difficult, whether necessarily so or not.)

3 If you are studying a course alongside this book, choose a similar passage from a book used in your course. The passage should be short but should contain one or more key ideas (e.g. 'class' in social science; 'growth' in biology).

Write notes explaining:

■ what the passage means as a whole;

■ what the key idea(s) mean(s).

Notes are personal

We all have our own ways of learning; no one else can learn for us. So it is with note-making. There is no one right way to take notes. As you develop your skills in brainstorming, probing and researching, you will gradually develop your own style of notes – one that suits you and your way of learning.

Notes also vary according to:

■ the subject;

■ the purpose;

■ the type of source (e.g. interview, textbook, radio programme);

■ the quality of your source (e.g. a well-organised textbook or a rambling interview).

You can build up and refine your own style of note-making by comparing it with the styles of other students. The ideal way to collect new ideas on note-making would be to participate in a brainstorming session with a group of other adult students. Unfortunately, I can't provide you with that opportunity; instead, I offer you a 'second-best' alternative: a dialogue between four fictional students. I hope that their ideas and comments are helpful to you. Compare what you do with what these students do.

A dialogue on making notes

Tony   *My notes vary according to what I'm doing. When I'm analysing the question I write down a few odd words and phrases – just to guide my thinking. Then I brainstorm and I use patterned notes for this: I enjoy filling the page, thinking of as much as I can. Then I pick out of my patterned notes the questions that I want to find answers to. I list these. I put one question on the top of each sheet of file paper. I then fill in the sheets as I come across answers in my books and other sources. When I've got all this information I decide on what is relevant to the question, cross out what's not and then list in order the points I want to make in the essay.*

Christine   *I don't set about collecting material in that way at all. When I find a good point I write it on a small piece of paper. (I tear up old paper, blank on one side, into bits – all the same size.) I make just one note on each sheet of paper together with a brief note of where I found the material. I keep a separate full note of the source – author, title, publisher, date of publication if it's a book. That way I can easily find out full details and don't need to write them out every time. When I have to plan the essay I shuffle the sheets around until I get them into what seems the best order for the question.*

John   *I like the convenience of having points on separate pieces of paper. But I buy cards from the stationer's and write one note on each card leaving plenty of space. Later on I put a letter or number on the top right hand side of each card to remind me where it comes in the order of the essay. I also add extra notes such as reminders to myself of how I plan to use that note or how it links in with others. And, like you Christine, I add a note of the source. I use a different size of card for this. Here's an example:*

note to help organise a
plan later

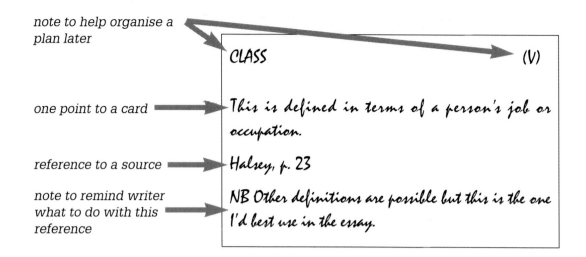

CLASS   (V)

one point to a card ➡ This is defined in terms of a person's job or occupation.

reference to a source ➡ Halsey, p. 23

note to remind writer
what to do with this
reference ➡ NB Other definitions are possible but this is the one I'd best use in the essay.

details of source on smaller card

author ➡ HALSEY, A H

title ➡ Change in British Society

details of edition
(found on inside page
of a book) ➡ Oxford UP, 2nd edition, 1981

Peter   I'm not nearly as organised as the rest of you. My notes are on all sorts of odd bits and pieces of paper, backs of envelopes, even receipts from shops. I just work in that way, a bit chaotic. And sometimes I lose them too. I've tried to be more organised but it's just me and the way I work.

Christine   I use an elastic band for my bits of paper. After all, if they're on cards you feel guilty about throwing them out and once I've done the essay I don't need the notes any more. I don't want expensive plastic boxes full of cards I don't want.

Tony   Yes, I think it's important to chuck notes out. My brother's got boxes and boxes of old notes, taken years ago. He never looks at them but he keeps them like lucky charms. He just can't bear to throw them out. My file sheets get cut up and re-stuck. I mount the relevant bits on new sheets of paper, in the order I want them to appear in the essay. Also, it's soothing and relaxing to use scissors and paste. It somehow frees my mind to think over my ideas and how I'm going to express them.

John   What worries me about my essays is that I can't seem to find enough to say. My notes are tidy but they never seem enough. I can't take my ideas further.

Christine   My problem's the opposite. I get all too easily led off the point into making notes for their own sake. I suppose I ought to keep my questions more clearly in my mind and collect answers only for them.

Peter   The problem with that is that new things suggest themselves as you go. You think of new questions or get into points that are relevant but which you never thought of.

Christine   *Yes – but I get tired, lose control and just start copying out of books!*

Tony   *That's the trouble. It's no good reading, or making notes when you're tired, though, is it? Because you can't think then.*

Peter   *I try to work out how the book is organised – I look at headings; tables and diagrams; any summaries, introductions or conclusions. That way I can find the bits relevant to me. I try to remind myself of what I know about the subject before reading any particular book or article. And I try to be critical of what the author has to say. After all, the author may be wrong or trying to persuade me to accept something without giving enough evidence. I try to spot points in the argument which are unclear or suspicious.*

4

a   Which of these students are you most like in your note-making? John, Christine, Tony or Peter?

b   Which of the students in the dialogue most clearly uses questions taken at the probing stage to guide later collection of material?

c   Which student says that he/she too easily forgets the questions to which he/she wants answers?

d   Which student goes for a general view of what's in a particular book, before working on it in more detail?

e   Which student says he/she always tries to be critical of what is in books?

f   Which students discuss the recording of sources?

(Use your A4 sheet.)

a   I can't of course answer this question for you.

b   Tony

c   Christine

d   Peter

e   Peter

f   Christine and John.

Check back to the dialogue if you were uncertain of any of the answers.

5

Peter says he wishes he could be more organised. John says he can't find enough to say. What advice would you give to help them?

Many answers are possible. It's difficult to know how to help without knowing more about the students. Perhaps Peter could carry a small notebook around everywhere with him? Perhaps he shouldn't worry too much about his disorganisation as he seems to make up for that by other strengths. John could try brainstorming; work at this stage often seems to help students who find it hard to think of things to say. Or he could meet with other students and ask them, through discussion, to help him take his ideas further.

Check your learning

1 List two purposes which notes may serve.

2 State two possible kinds of source a writer might consult when collecting material for an essay.

3 Why is it necessary to state the sources of ideas/facts?

4 Why is it important to use your own words when making notes? (Give one reason.)

5 Why is there no one single best way of making notes? (Give one reason.)

6 List at least two different ways of making notes mentioned during the dialogue between Christine, Peter, Tony and John.

Read on only when you have answered the questions yourself.

Answers

1 See the discussion of SAQ 1.

2 Books, people, yourself, radio programmes, television programmes. (There are many other possible sources.)

3 To enable your reader to check details, find out more, assess the value of the information, check your ability to use sources.

4 If you work on rephrasing ideas and information in your own words, then you are much more likely to understand and remember what's in your notes. By struggling to express ideas, you make them your own.

5 Notes vary according to the individual making them, the purpose the notes are serving, the subject being studied.

6 Patterned notes; lists of points; small pieces of paper; cards; odd sheets, e.g. shop bills. Other answers are possible; if you are in doubt about yours, check back to the dialogue.

UNIT
6

PLANNING

What this unit is about

This is the first of two units covering the planning stage of essay writing. By the time you have finished your work on this unit, you should be able to:

→ explain why it is important to plan;

→ show how planning can be carried out in a variety of ways;

→ explain how the essay plan is based on the key verbs in the essay title.

Planning in daily life

Most of us organise our time by making lists. We plan what we're going to do each day, to save time and to make sure things get done. We may plan:

■ chronologically, by drawing up a schedule for the day:

> 9.00   Take the dog for a walk
>
> 9.30   Read two chapters of my set book
>
> 10.30 Clean the house

■ according to activities or tasks, by listing what we hope to accomplish in the day:

> Clean the house
>
> Read two chapters of my set book
>
> Take the dog for a walk

■ according to priorities, by listing the day's activities in order of importance:

> 1   Read two chapters of my set book
>
> 2   Take the dog for a walk
>
> 3   Clean the house

1 How do you plan a typical day? Chronologically, by activity, or according to priorities? Or do you have a different way?

Planning an essay

What does this sort of everyday planning have to do with writing essays? You plan your day so that you use your time efficiently, and nothing essential is forgotten. The same reasons apply to planning an essay. If you plan your essay carefully:

- you won't waste your time on points or ideas that aren't essential;

- you will embark on writing your essay with a clear sense of what needs to be done;

- you will be sure that you have dealt with all the important aspects of the question.

At the planning stage of an essay the writer reads critically all the information collected earlier and sorts it out. The writer summarises, expands, rearranges, makes corrections. The end product of this stage is a plan – a guide to the final essay. Let's look at the example I have taken earlier:

'Society today is totally different from society in 1900.' Evaluate this statement.

A student working on this essay will probably have collected a lot of material on a whole variety of topics. The material will be unsorted. There may be information on:

— housing	— sport and leisure	— food
— health	— marriage	— clothing
— education	— place of women in the home	— costs of various goods and services
— quality of life		
— hobbies	— role of the family	— pollution
— work	— television and radio	— pace of life
— place of women at work	— advent of microcomputers	— rise of new industries
— longer life expectancy	— higher expectations	— speed of communication
	— control of disease	
— transport	— political institutions	— banking and insurance
— child rearing		
— care of the elderly	— laws	— divorce

The student would also have made brief notes on what the essay title requires. (Remember this process was discussed in Unit 3, 'Analysing the question: key verbs and key ideas'.)

At the planning stage, you must decide which points to develop and which to discard. It's very rare that you can get everything in; you have to learn to throw some away. You stand back, select the most promising material and decide how to group it into 'chunks'. In most essays it is possible to deal with only about four chunks of material.

Can you see ways to group the points on page 44 into four chunks? (Remember that you won't be able to deal with all the information.) Spend some time on this – cover up the response below until you have finished.

There are many ways to organise this material. (You will nearly always find that several options are open to you at the planning stage.) The following list shows one possible way to select four chunks of information from the list of points.

MATERIAL DIFFERENCES
- housing
- clothing
- costs of various goods and services
- food

CHANGES TO INSTITUTIONS
- commercial (banks and insurance)
- education (schools, colleges, universities)
- political
- legal

CHANGES IN EMPLOYMENT
- old industries dying (e.g. rail, heavy engineering)
- new industries rising (e.g. electronics, microcomputers)
- women's work (e.g. service industries)

GENERAL CHANGES: VALUES, ETC.
- expectations differ
- pace of life faster
- pollution

Please note that this is a simplified example of an essay plan. A student at this stage of planning would normally have much more information to work with – e.g. some examples of pollution, some statistics on the changing costs of goods and services, etc.

Check back to the original list on page 44. What has not been included
a in your plan?
b in my plan?

a   I cannot answer this for you, but you should have a careful look yourself.

b   In my plan, I left out health, hobbies, longer life expectancy, transport, child rearing, care of the elderly, sport and leisure, marriage, role of the family, television and radio, control of disease, speed of communication, divorce.

An alternative way of grouping points would be:

■ use of leisure (sport; hobbies);

■ marriage and family (marriage; role of the family; divorce; child rearing; care of the elderly);

■ medical (health; care of disease; longer life expectancy);

■ communications (new methods of transport and communication).

Your choice of points and groupings will depend both on your subject and on your level of study.

Writing an essay is the act of pulling together many bits of information into a coherent argument or presentation. It is at the planning stage that you decide how to accomplish this. You want to present your reader with something that's clear and easy to read, not with a mass of apparently unrelated points. The truly effective writer is not one who has 'facts', but one who knows how to use facts in an organised way.

How people plan essays

Each person will set about planning in a way that suits him or herself. We saw in the last unit that this was true, too, of making notes. Let's look at the students we met earlier. How do they plan their essays?

Peter   *I plan my essays in my head, often largely on the bus on my way to work. I find I plan best when I'm away from all my books and notes. A pattern sort of evolves. I get that pattern clear and then go back to my notes. I ditch points which don't fit the pattern. I've got quite ruthless about this – if I try to get too much in then the shape of the essay is wrong and I get criticised for it being 'badly structured'.*

 Look back at what Tony says about note-making in the last unit. Are there any clues on how he plans his essays?

He tells us that he organises the material he collects onto sheets of file paper, according to the question he is asking. Then, later, he looks at the question and crosses out what is not relevant. He then lists the points he wants to make. This list is a plan; presumably he consults it as he writes up the essay and it refers him back to the appropriate parts of his file.

Later on he tells us that sometimes he cuts his file sheets up and sticks them on fresh pieces of paper, in the order he wants to use them for the essay. This is another kind of planning.

 Now look back to what Christine says. How does she plan her essays?

She uses small sheets of paper for note-making. When she's collected her material she re-shuffles the pieces of paper until they're in the right order for the essay. (Presumably she also throws out some of her sheets; not all the material she has collected would be relevant.)

 Is John's method of planning likely to be closer to Tony's or to Christine's?

His method is closer to Christine's. John too would be likely to use the 'shuffling' method with his cards. Note that both John and Christine write only one point on each piece of paper, so that they can arrange the points independently.

So we have seen that planning can take various forms, depending on the individual's preference and temperament. Some people are more methodical than others; some people like lists and others like patterns.

Turn back to my answer to SAQ 2 in this unit. Let's look at different ways of drawing up a plan for this set of points.

Plan 1

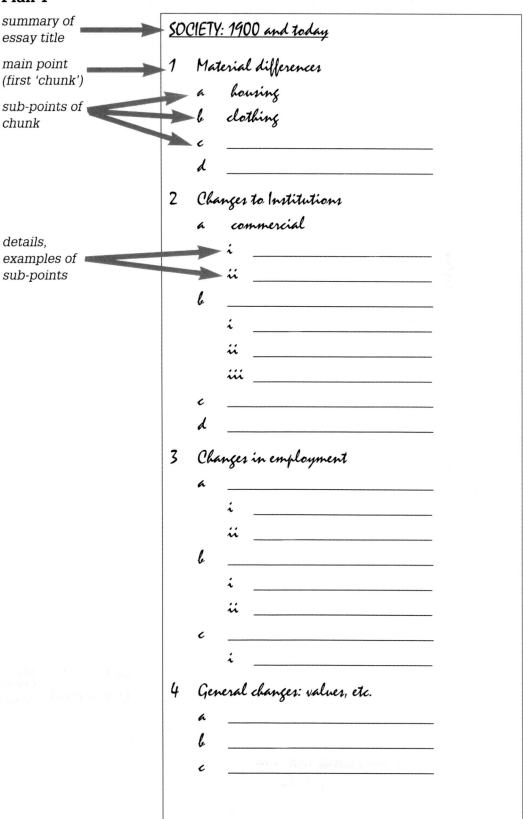

summary of essay title → **SOCIETY: 1900 and today**

main point (first 'chunk') → 1 Material differences

sub-points of chunk →
  a   housing
  b   clothing
  c   _____
  d   _____

2 Changes to Institutions
  a   commercial

details, examples of sub-points →
      i   _____
      ii _____
  b   _____
      i   _____
      ii _____
      iii _____
  c   _____
  d   _____

3 Changes in employment
  a   _____
      i   _____
      ii _____
  b   _____
      i   _____
      ii _____
  c   _____
      i   _____

4 General changes: values, etc.
  a   _____
  b   _____
  c   _____

First, note details of the layout (the arrows and labels help you to see this). The nearer the points are to the left hand side of the page the more important they are. This plan is basically in the form of a list.

I have deliberately left spaces in Plan 1. Complete the plan (i.e. fill in the entries for 1c and d, 2a, i and ii, b, c and d; all the points under headings 3 and 4).

SOCIETY: 1900 and today

1 Material differences
   a   housing
   b   clothing
   c   costs of goods and services
   d   food

2 Changes to institutions
   a   commercial
      i   banks
      ii insurance
   b   education
      i   schools
      ii colleges
      iii universities
   c   political
   d   legal

3 Changes in employment
   a   old industries dying
      i   rail
      ii heavy engineering
   b   new industries rising
      i   microcomputer
      ii electronics
   c   women's work
      i   service industries

4 General changes: values, etc.
   a   expectations differ
   b   pace of life faster
   c   pollution

Plan 2 shows another way of setting out exactly the same information.

Plan 2

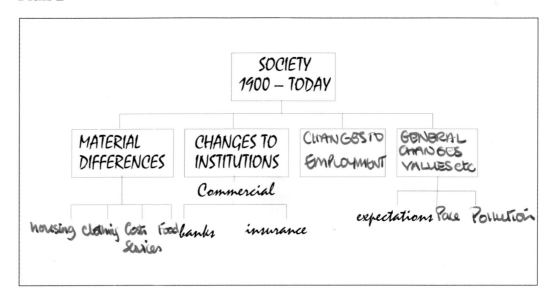

This type of plan is called a tree diagram. The points are arranged in order of importance – the more important the point the higher up the page. Some students like this method because it shows visually how the points relate one to the other.

8 If you would like practice in working with a tree diagram, I suggest that you fill in the blank spaces in Plan 2, so that the diagram contains the same information as the list in SAQ 2.

You can also use a form of patterned notes, as seen in Plan 3.

Plan 3

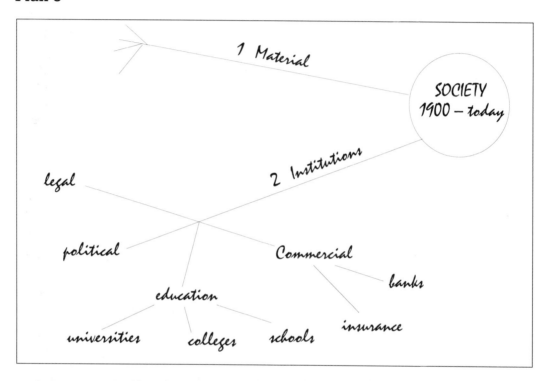

9 If you would like practice in working with patterned notes, complete Plan 3 to include the points made in the other essay plans.

Choosing a planning method

I have shown you three ways to plan an essay, but there are of course many other ways to organise your information. For example, you could use a simplified list, without all the numbers and indented headings of the first plan. You could also use a completely different approach, such as the sheets of paper that Christine uses. Choose a method that suits you. The planning method you use isn't important. What matters is that you do go through the process of planning – that you sort your material so that:

■ you know how to use it in your essay;

■ your completed essay makes sense to your reader.

Whatever method you decide to use (and I hope you will experiment with various methods), make sure that your plan:

■ shows the sequence of points to be covered;

■ has a clear structure, showing the relative importance of one point to another.

10 Look back to the three plans. Does each plan meet these two conditions of sequence and structure? If so, how?

They all show sequence and structure, but in different ways. Plan 1 sets out the points in order; the relative importance of points one to the other is made clear by headings, use of numbers and letters, and use of indentation (i.e. how near the points are to the left hand side of the page). Plan 2 is sequenced left to right and shows the structure by means of a diagram. Plan 3 is similarly diagrammatic: the branches off the lines clearly show which are main points and which are secondary points. Plan 3 numbers the main points to indicate sequence.

Key verbs again

The kind of plan you make will depend partly on the key verb contained in (or implied by) the question. We looked at key verbs in Unit 3. The following SAQ which relates key verbs to essay plans, uses the same sample questions as SAQ 6, on page 21 of Unit 3. (You might refer back now to pages 24-5, just to review briefly key verbs.)

11 The sample essay questions in Unit 3 were based on this statement: 'Society today is totally different from society in 1900.' Four different key verbs produced four different questions:

a Justify this statement.

b Outline the main stages of change.

c Evaluate this statement.

d Diagnose the main causes of change.

How would the key verb in each question influence the essay plan? I will do (a) for you as an example.

a **Justify:** The plan would need to include points to support the statement.

b **Outline:** The plan would need to divide the period 1900 to today into four or five sub-periods to show the main stages of change:

1900–1914	Years of calm
1914–1930	War and its aftermath
1930–1950	Depression and war again
1950–1970	Industrial change
1970–today	The silicon chip and its consequences

c **Evaluate:** This is the question I've been using for various examples in the book. The writer's judgement of the degree of truth in the question is wanted. Material would have to be planned in such a way that this judgement clearly emerged (e.g. points for, points against, conclusion stressing points for).

d **Diagnose:** The essay would need to explain the main causes, grouped in chunks (e.g. economic, cultural, industrial) and perhaps organised in increasing order of importance.

You can see now how important it is to analyse the question (Unit 3). Analysing the key verbs and key ideas in the essay question is essential groundwork for drawing up your essay plan.

Check your learning

1   Give two reasons why planning is important.

2   Why is it important to discard some material you have collected when you come to the planning stage?

3   There are several ways of setting out plans. Name any two mentioned in this unit.

4   How might plans for the following two essay topics differ? (You might find it helpful to consult the list of key verbs on pages 24-5 of Unit 3.)

    a Define community.

    b Describe the community in which you live.

Read on only when you have answered the questions yourself.

Answers

1   It makes a well shaped essay more likely.

It makes writing the essay easier.

It helps you to get the main points clear.

It helps the reader to take in your ideas.

2   In an essay of (say) 1500 words, you can discuss only a limited number of points. It's much better to make a few points thoroughly than to discuss a large number of points inadequately. You will also find that it's difficult to arrange a large number of points in a clear and logical sequence.

3   In your head (Peter); a list (Tony); cutting and sticking (Tony); shuffling sheets or cards (John and Christine); tree diagram; patterned notes.

4   Topic (a) requires a discussion of the meaning of community. The plan would need to give several definitions and settle for one; or discuss various aspects of one major definition.

Topic (b) expects a detailed account of the main features of one particular community.

PARAGRAPHING

What this unit is about

This is the second of two units on the planning stage of essay writing. It deals with how to plan and link paragraphs.

By the time you have finished your work on this unit, you should be able to:

→ relate the planning stage to the writing of paragraphs;

→ list the main ingredients of a paragraph;

→ identify and write clear topic sentences;

→ support topic sentences in a variety of ways;

→ identify and use 'signposting' words and phrases;

→ explain the importance of good paragraphing and signposting.

The planning stage and writing paragraphs

Planning for an essay should take place at three levels, as Figure 7.1 illustrates.

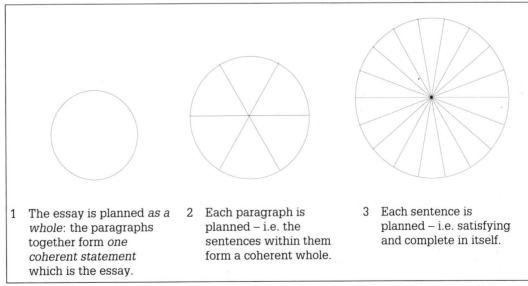

1 The essay is planned *as a whole*: the paragraphs together form *one coherent statement* which is the essay.

2 Each paragraph is planned – i.e. the sentences within them form a coherent whole.

3 Each sentence is planned – i.e. satisfying and complete in itself.

Figure 7.1 Three stages in essay planning

We discussed the first level in Unit 6. The third level – planning for sentences – will be covered in Unit 10. In this unit we will focus on the second level: the planning and linking of paragraphs.

The best way to learn to write is to read widely and write often. For some lucky students, this is enough: they learn to write paragraphs quite painlessly. But for most of us, paragraphing presents real difficulties. This unit suggests a simple method for constructing paragraphs. While in the short run it may produce rather mechanical writing, it *can* help you to develop a sense of how a paragraph should be put together.

You may find that you just cannot write according to a method. If this is the case, then use the method as a kind of checklist; go back over the paragraphs you have drafted to ensure that they do have all the necessary elements.

The fuller and more careful your plan the easier paragraphing is. If you look back to the plans in Unit 6 you'll see that the section on material differences (in our sample essay on changing society) could contain paragraphs on housing, clothing, costs and food. Or these could be amalgamated into, say, one or two paragraphs. Either way the plan leads the writer logically and straightforwardly to build the paragraphs.

What is a paragraph?

What are the ingredients of a successful paragraph? The approach I shall take is that each paragraph should contain one clear controlling idea and sentences which provide support to this controlling idea.

The length of paragraphs depends on a number of things – the subject matter, the point being made, the writer's style. It is not possible to specify length, though in practice to think of four, five or six sentences is a very rough guide. Better to ask yourself of every paragraph you write:

- Is there one main idea here?

- Is it stated clearly?

- Is it properly supported?

- Does it link neatly with the previous paragraph and anticipate the next?

The topic sentence

The controlling idea is usually expressed in what is sometimes called the topic sentence, a sentence (usually – but not always – placed at the start of the paragraph) which makes clear the point the paragraph is to discuss. The topic sentence summarises the content of the paragraph and sets up the terms within which the paragraph will remain. Look at the following example.

> Standards of housing improved considerably during the period. At the turn of the century 60% of the population lived in houses which would, today, be considered unfit for habitation. Overcrowding was common and led to other problems, such as inadequate sanitation and the transmission of disease. Building regulations were either non-existent or not enforced. The situation is very different today.

(The statistics are invented. In a real-life example, a source would be given for these.)

1 Which is the topic sentence? (As always use your A4 sheet to hide my responses throughout this unit.)

The first sentence is the topic sentence: it sets up the point which the remainder of the paragraph explores.

 Which of the following would be an acceptable alternative topic sentence for the paragraph we have just discussed?

a   Poor houses can be built at any date.

b   Housing in 1900 was often of much lower quality than today.

The paragraph is making the point that housing today is superior (in many ways) to housing in 1900. Sentence (b) conveys the same controlling idea as the topic sentence in the original. Sentence (a) does not make this point at all and would make nonsense if put at the beginning of the sample paragraph.

 a   What might the next paragraph cover?

b   Give a reason for your answer.

a   The next paragraph would probably outline aspects of housing today.

b   The last sentence makes links to housing today. (We'll look later at links between paragraphs.)

 The following paragraph is jumbled up. The sentences are deliberately out of order. Underline the topic sentence.

These can then be used as the basis for school work. Admittedly there are sometimes criticisms of this newer approach. They are encouraged too to bring into the school interests and concerns of the home and playground – a new baby in the family, games and hobbies. Children are taught not only to read, write and add up but also to paint, to play music and to explore their surroundings. Whereas in 1900 a public elementary school taught only the 'three Rs', its current equivalent, the state primary, has a much wider curriculum.

You should have underlined 'Whereas in 1900 a public elementary school taught only the "three Rs", its current equivalent, the state primary, has a much wider curriculum'. The controlling idea of the paragraph is the way in which the school curriculum has broadened during the century. The topic sentence must clearly express this controlling idea. (We shall return to this sample paragraph later.)

 Read the paragraph below. Does this meet the requirements I have outlined for a good paragraph? Is there one main idea? Is it clearly stated in the topic sentence?

There have been major changes in transportation and information can now be communicated instantaneously. People go by car when they used to go by horse drawn vehicle. Clerks used to take information from one office to another but this is no longer necessary. Air travel puts foreign countries within easy reach of Britain.

It seems to me rather confused. There are two ideas (though they are related) and the topic sentence tries to state them both at once.

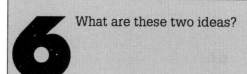

What are these two ideas?

There have been major changes in transportation and there have been major changes in the communication of information. These two ideas would, I think, be better separated into two paragraphs

Write two paragraphs based on these two main ideas. Give each paragraph a clear topic sentence. Add to, or change, any of the details as you feel necessary.

There are obviously many ways to answer this question. The following sample paragraphs demonstrate one way to develop the main ideas of transportation and communication. The topic sentence in each paragraph indicates clearly what the paragraph will be about. (Notice that the first paragraph leads into the second; see the response to SAQ 3 above.)

> There have been major changes in transportation. Where once people travelled on foot or by horse they now use motor vehicles. 70% of all families now own a car and 40% own two cars. High speed inter-city trains and domestic air services mean that business people can travel to a day's work two or three hundred miles away. Air travel puts foreign countries within easy reach of one another. These changes have been accompanied by parallel developments in the transmission of information.
>
> Information today can be communicated almost instantaneously from one office to another. Developments in electronics have made this possible. In 1900 messenger boys or clerks used to travel in person, with attache cases full of documents; today this is almost unknown. When once it was necessary to wait two or three days for a letter to arrive, decisions can now be given across the telephone or via computers. Such developments do, though, have their drawbacks.

Note again the way the final sentence in the first paragraph leads forward to the subject matter of the next.

The statistics in this example are invented. Please remember that for a real essay on this topic, sources would have to be provided for any statistical information. For example:

> 70% of all families now own a car and 40% own two cars. (Attwood, p.84.)

The advantages of clear topic sentences both for the writer and for the reader need to be stressed.

For the writer

The topic sentence is clear guidance as to exactly what should go into the paragraph.

For the reader

The topic sentence helps the reader to see quickly what point is to be made in the paragraph. It prepares the reader for what follows; the route through the paragraph is clear from the start.

Support sentences

The topic sentence in a paragraph sets out the controlling idea. It is supported by the sentences which follow, each of which should in some way add to the topic sentence. These sentences may, for example, explain ideas raised in the topic sentence, define terms more fully, give supporting detail. Let's look at some examples. First turn back to the paragraph on standards of housing (page 54).

 How do the second, third, fourth and fifth sentences support the topic sentence?

Sentence 2: statistics to back up the topic sentence

Sentence 3: defines 'unfit for habitation' – overcrowding, inadequate sanitation

Sentence 4: gives a reason for poor standards in 1900

Sentence 5: emphasises that the situation has changed

 Turn back now to the paragraph which had its sentences out of sequence (in SAQ 4). There you picked out the topic sentence. First, write out this topic sentence. Next, put the sentences in an order that makes sense, to support this topic sentence.

This is the order I would choose:

> Whereas in 1900 a public elementary school taught only the 'three Rs', today its equivalent, the state primary, has a much wider curriculum. Children are taught not only to read, write and add up but also to paint, to play music and to explore their surroundings. They are encouraged too to bring unto the school interests and concerns of the home and playground – a new baby in the family, games and hobbies. These can then be used as the basis for school work. Admittedly there are sometimes criticisms of this newer approach.

Note the way in which each of the sentences supports the controlling idea of the paragraph, contained in the first sentence. If your order is different (which it may be) you are not necessarily 'wrong'; just check that your paragraph hangs together.

A special kind of support sentence is one which concludes a paragraph or anticipates the next. Not all paragraphs will need this, but a sentence which either sums up what the paragraph has said or which leads on to the next paragraph (or even does both) is sometimes helpful – though a concluding sentence should not simply repeat the topic sentence.

10 Write down two examples of sentences, from the paragraphs on the 'society' topic given in this unit, that anticipate the topic of the next paragraph.

Here are four examples:

> Standards of housing improved considerably during the period. At the turn of the century 60% of the population lived in houses which would, today, be considered unfit for habitation. Overcrowding was common and led to other problems, such as inadequate sanitation and the transmission of disease. Building regulations were either non-existent or not enforced. The situation is very different today.

The final sentence of this paragraph, 'The situation is very different today', both concludes the paragraph and moves clearly on to a discussion of housing today.

The final sentence of this paragraph both links to points covered earlier in the paragraph ('These changes…') and leads directly on to the paragraph that will follow (on the transmission of information).

> There have been major changes in transportation. Where once people travelled on foot or by horse they now use motor vehicles. 70% of families now own a car and 40% own two cars. High speed inter-city trains and domestic air services mean that business people can travel to a day's work two or three hundred miles away. Air travel puts foreign countries within easy reach of one another. These changes have been accompanied by parallel developments in the transmission of information.

> Information today can be communicated almost instantaneously from one office to another. Developments in electronics have made this possible. In 1900 messenger boys or clerks used to travel in person, with attache cases full of documents; today this is almost unknown. When once it was necessary to wait two or three days for a letter to arrive, decisions can now be given across the telephone or via computers. Such developments do, though, have their drawbacks.

Here, the final sentence clearly refers forward to the subject of the next paragraph ('drawbacks').

> *Whereas in 1900 a public elementary school taught only the 'three Rs', today its equivalent, the state primary, has a much wider curriculum. Children are taught not only to read, write and add up but also to paint, to play music and to explore their surroundings. They are encouraged too to bring unto the school interests and concerns of the home and playground – a new baby in the family, games and hobbies. These can then be used as the basis for school work. Admittedly there are sometimes criticisms of this newer approach.*

Again, this paragraph indicates in its final sentence that the next topic for discussion will be 'criticisms of this newer approach'.

Examples

Support sentences often include examples which help the reader to grasp the controlling idea of the paragraph. We all need illustrations, details, concrete examples before we can 'see the point'; ideas can pass over the head of a reader unless they are grounded in reality.

11 Look back to the fourth paragraph discussed in the response to SAQ10, which discussed changes in education. Are examples used in the support sentences?

Yes, examples of the wider curriculum are given: paint, music, explore surroundings. Examples of interests and activities outside school are used: new baby, games, hobbies.

12 Look back to the second and third paragraphs in SAQ 10 (dealing with transportation and communication respectively). Are examples used in the support sentences?

Examples of changes in transportation: foot/horse to motor vehicles, high speed train and air travel.

Examples of changes in communication: messenger boys and letters to telephones and computers.

In this unit so far, I have stressed the value of coherent paragraphs. One way to make sure that your paragraphs are coherent is to start off with a topic sentence that states the controlling idea, and then follow it with support sentences which elaborate the topic sentence and provide examples. The advantage of tackling paragraph writing in this way is that it forces you to attend to the structure of what you want to say; a clear structure makes the reader's job so much easier. When you have written a paragraph, read it carefully (aloud, if possible) to spot any imbalance (e.g. too many or too few ideas; not enough support; no clear controlling idea; no examples). If you're unsure, ask a friend or fellow student to check.

Signposting

I referred earlier to the importance of clear topic sentences and also to concluding or anticipatory support sentences. These devices are part of the way in which you signpost your reader around the material. Signposting words and phrases explain what you are about to discuss, and link what you have said with what you are going on to say. They help your reader to follow the structure of your argument; at critical points you show your reader what you are planning to do and why. They may be single words ('however', 'but', 'similarly') or sentences.

13 Reread the concluding sentences of the second, third and fourth paragraphs listed in the response to SAQ 10. Pick out words which signpost the reader and say which refer backwards to what has been covered, and which refer

First paragraph: 'These changes...' refers backward; the rest of the sentence leads the reader forward.

Second paragraph: 'Such developments...' refers backward; the rest of the sentence leads the reader forward.

Third paragraph: 'This' refers backward; the rest of the sentence leads forward.

14 Underline, or write out, the signposting words and phrases in the following examples:

a   In the next few paragraphs I will briefly outline the causes of hurricanes.

b   I will look in turn at fish farming, market gardening and domestic heating and examine the particular features of each.

c   And television is certainly entertaining.

a   *In the next few paragraphs I will briefly outline* the causes of hurricanes.

b   *I will look in turn at* fish farming, market gardening and domestic heating *and examine the particular features of each.*

c   *And* television is certainly entertaining.

You may have underlined slightly different words; the important thing here is to distinguish the *content* – fish farming, hurricanes, etc. – from the words which show how the author is going to handle the content – the signposting words. You may have recalled a similar distinction made in Unit 3 between content words and key verbs – the latter are signposts to you, the writer, on how the content is to be handled.

You may also have recalled the points I made in Unit 2 about the differences between speaking and writing. I said that in writing we have to find ways of conveying some of the guidance and emphasis which we achieve in speech by our pace, tone and gestures. Signposting is one of these ways.

Look out for signposting words and phrases in the books, newspapers and magazines you read. Use them where appropriate in your own writing.

If you want to learn more about signposting techniques, *How to Succed in Exams and Assessments*, another publication in this series, might be helpful. Information on this and other useful references is in Appendix 4, 'Further reading'.

Check your learning

1 What advantage does a clear topic sentence have

    a   for the reader?

    b   for the writer?

2 Re-read the two paragraphs supplied as a sample for SAQ 7. Do the sentences in each paragraph adequately support the controlling idea as expressed in the topic sentences?

3 Why bother so much about paragraphing? (Give one reason.)

4 Check through part of this book. Write down some examples of signposting words and phrases.

Read on only when you have answered the questions yourself. Use your A4 sheet.

Answers

1 It helps the reader to identify the points of the paragraph; it helps the writer in selecting material for the paragraph.

2 I hope so. They are intended to! Check other paragraphs (e.g. in books and papers) and analyse them in the way suggested in this unit. (Sometimes, though, experienced writers construct paragraphs more flexibly.)

3 The main reason is that good paragraphing helps the reader to follow the ideas in your essay. You may have written something similar or you may have found another reason such as 'students are often not very confident in writing paragraphs'.

4 There are plenty in the book. Here are some examples from this unit:

> *In this unit we will focus on… the planning and linking of paragraphs.*

> *This unit suggests a simple method for constructing paragraphs.*

> *Look at the following example.*

> *(We shall return to this sample paragraph later.)*

> *Let's look at some examples. First turn back to the paragraph on standards of housing.*

There are many other examples, both in this unit and in the book as a whole.

UNIT 8

DRAFTING AND CHECKING

What this unit is about

In this unit we move from the planning stage to the drafting stage. (You might want to refer back to Unit 2 to refresh your memory about the four stages of the writing process.)

By the time you finish your work on this unit, you should be able to:

→ explain the advantages of writing a rough draft of your essay;

→ follow a procedure for drafting and checking your work.

Drafting

At the drafting stage, you revise, reconsider and rewrite what you have already produced and write fresh sections as necessary. If your work in planning and paragraphing has been thorough then you may not have very much to do. You will have structured the essay, getting the sequence of points right, and you will have translated this detailed plan into paragraphs.

But not everybody works as logically as that. I know I don't. More probably you'll have some parts of the essay relatively well organised but others less so. Or you may only have sketched out your paragraphs, deciding to write them out in full later. You may have left detailed paragraphing altogether until you have made a rough draft direct from your plan. In this sense the stages I have outlined are flexible and each one of us will work differently. You will probably find yourself shuttling backwards and forwards across the stages.

The drafting stage is where you put the essay together, reviewing all the work you have done earlier and filling in any gaps (e.g. sections still to be written). The amount of drafting you need to do will depend on such things as:

■ how you have tackled earlier stages;

■ how difficult the topic is;

■ how right you want the finished essay to be.

Let's pause for a moment over this last point. You can aim at 'getting by', at writing an essay that is just adequate. Sometimes we do just want to get an essay out of the way, because we are busy, or bored with the topic. On other occasions we really want to do full justice to an essay title. Then we may progress by drafting and checking, and going through these sequences several times.

One important point: drafting is a stage in learning. As we draft, we also understand our topic more clearly, and all the time we are developing our writing skills.

Some people say that they don't need to write drafts. But although they may not actually put pen to paper these people almost certainly do draft – in their heads. If work at earlier stages has been thoroughly carried out, and if you know the topic thoroughly, then it is possible to work out the ideas, in sequence, mentally.

But most of us *need* to draft. I can carry out some of the work in my head but I *always* need to sit down and rough out the essay. Why do I bother with a rough copy?

■ The rough copy shows me what I need to work further on. (As a student using an earlier version of this book said: 'I make a rough copy first and then read it through a day later. It's amazing all the problems I pick up.')

■ In the rough copy I can try out various approaches, crossing out those that don't lead anywhere.

Writing drafts helps me to get going; it produces work I can refine later.

 Write down two advantages of making a rough copy or draft of an essay. Cover up my response with the A4 sheet.

Several answers are possible. You may have two of the following (or others of your own):

■ It's rare that essays come out right first time.

■ It gives you more time on the essay and so you might phrase some of the more complex points more tellingly or lucidly.

■ You will produce a much tidier end product: as will be argued later (in Unit 11), presentation is important.

■ It helps many people to separate the stage of getting ideas down on paper from the stage of checking the detail of the English.

■ It avoids clumsy and confused sentences, because you can go back over the draft and make changes before the reader sees it.

■ It needn't take long because the draft is for your eyes only.

■ It helps learning to occur (e.g. understanding the topic; practising writing skills).

■ It helps you to try out a variety of approaches to a subject.

The process of drafting: an example

Let's follow through a student working on the essay about changing society. Just to remind you, the title of the essay is:

'Society today is totally different from society in 1900.' Evaluate this statement.

The student is working on the second section of the plan given under SAQ 2 of Unit 6. She takes a piece of paper, and divides the page into two, and working from her plan she writes a first draft in the right-hand column of the page, as shown opposite. (The other half of the page is blank):

Marriage in 1900 was sacred, you just didn't get divorced. People thought of marriage as a bond that could never be broken. It was all bound up with the family – another unit which was seen as sacred and unchangeable – probably a hangover from Victorian days. Divorce was avoided like the plague. It was a dirty word. People went to any lengths however great to avoid the scandal of divorce.

But there were some better things then about the family. People did look after the old better – often in the same street, though this was a matter of social class.

Now things have changed. Divorce is much more common (statistics here). There's not much stigma attached to being 'divorced' or 'separated'; single parent families are on the up. Family life has changed in lots of ways – more mobile, more flexible, each member tries to do more, women's role is more fluid, children are out more, other people take over family responsibilities (child minders, schools, play groups).

Why do you think she has left half the page blank?

So she can amend, alter, annotate what she has written. The student wrote all this down quickly, knowing she could come back and polish it later. She is concentrating on the content knowing that style and structure will be checked later.

This approach to drafting is taken from *How A Writer Works* by Roger Garrison; for more information on this book see Appendix 4, 'Further reading'.

The student writes notes in the blank half of the page, to help her carry out the next draft. The notes she made are shown on the next page:

Marginal notes (left column):

E   Expression, but deal with this later

2 separate paras here? One on divorce, one on the family?

good – linking words

build up family in 1900. too short – build up

find statistics

write separate paras on divorce, family life

I'm getting better here

Draft text (right column):

E Marriage in 1900 was sacred, you just didn't get divorced. People thought of marriage as a bond that could never be broken. *E* It was all bound up with the family – another unit which was seen as sacred and unchangeable – probably a hangover from Victorian days. Divorce was avoided like the plague. It was a dirty word. People went to any lengths however great to avoid the scandal of divorce.

E But there were some better things then about the family. People did look after the old better – often in the same street, though this was a matter of social class.

Now things have changed. Divorce is much more common (statistics here). There's not much stigma attached to being 'divorced' or 'separated'; single parent families are on the up. Family *E* life has changed in lots of ways – more mobile, more flexible, each member tries to do more, women's role is more fluid, children are out more, other people take over family responsibilities (child minders, schools, play groups).

The student is checking logic, sequence and structure with the needs of the reader in mind. What I think has happened is that, as often when drafting, she has gradually written herself into the topic. She gets under way at the end, when she writes about the modern family. This causes her, on re-reading, to want to reorganise earlier material to get a balance. She has also picked out some structural weaknesses. The first paragraph deals with two topics (do you remember the communication example I gave in the last unit?); the second paragraph is too short. She needs to go back and reshape her material. Notice that she also identifies the strengths in her draft – the linking words and the ending.

In a further draft the student could put right the weaknesses, using the advice on paragraph structure given in the last unit. She also has noticed some problems in expression (marked *E*), but will deal with these later.

Let's summarise the drafting process this student has used:

1   Write a rough draft, concentrating on the content and on getting down your ideas as freely as possible.

2 Check what you write (using the split page technique if you wish). Ask yourself:

- Are ideas in the right sequence?

- Does the essay have structure?

- Will the reader follow the logic I am using?

- Do I need to find more information?

- Am I paragraphing coherently?

- Am I signposting my reader?

(This will involve going over the work you have carried out at earlier stages.)

3 Then amend as necessary. (I use 'scissors and paste': I cut out bits that seem in the wrong place and paste them up in a more suitable position. A wordprocessor is ideal for this, if you have one.)

Work on your essay until it is clearly structured, with good paragraphs and links.

As a student using an earlier version of this book wrote:

> I have to check my rough draft very carefully. I'm sometimes so clear in my own mind about what I want to say that I just don't make it clear enough to a tutor. I get my rough draft read by a friend – he tells me what's confusing.

The final stages of checking – when you correct any errors in expression, check spelling and punctuation, and prepare the final copy of the essay, as discussed in Units 10 and 11.

You may think, 'What a rigmarole! I haven't time to go through all those stages'. But the experience of many students has been that, in the end, to go through this sequence saves time and leads to better results. You do, of course, have to schedule rather carefully the time you have got. The mind seems to benefit from having just one job to carry out at a time. Once you have practised this process, you'll find it takes no longer than more conventional ways of working. I suggest that you give it a try – or several tries, as you will probably not discover all the benefits first time round.

Check your learning

1 List two advantages to writing a rough draft.

2 What do you need to look for when you check a rough draft?

Read on only when you have answered the questions yourself. Use the A4 sheet.

Answers

1 Review the answers supplied for SAQ 1.

2 The sequence of ideas; structure; logic; paragraphing; signposting; whether more information is needed. (You may also have mentioned checking the English, an activity I cover in Unit 10.)

UNIT 9

INTRODUCTIONS AND CONCLUSIONS

What this unit is about

I have deliberately left the writing of introductions and conclusions until now, i.e. until after the main body of the essay has been developed. Some writers leave till last the preparation of these parts of the essay; if you prefer to write them earlier, then it's still important to check them very carefully again later.

By the time you have finished your work on this unit, you should be able to:

→ recognise and write a sound introduction;

→ recognise and write a sound conclusion;

→ allow for introductions and conclusions when planning your essays.

Introductions

In the introduction you should state very clearly the way in which you are going to discuss the topic and the scope of the treatment. The introduction should make the reader want to read on, with a clear understanding of what the essay will contain. In addition a good introduction will show the writer 'means business' (by directly addressing the question).

1 Which of the following introductions seems most effective? Why? The essay title is:

'Society today is totally different from society in 1900.'
Evaluate this statement.

a *This statement is largely justified; there have been major changes between society in 1900 and society today. I shall explore four main areas of change: transport, health, education and family life. In each of these change has occurred through technological development and economic pressure.*

b *In some ways society is the same; in other ways it has changed. It is hard to know whether or not to agree with the statement. There have certainly been some changes.*

Please remember that this essay question is artificial, in that we don't know the course from which it is taken. It is an all-purpose title, deliberately chosen because I hope the subject is intelligible to all readers of this book, whatever course they happen to be studying.

I think (a) is better than (b). Paragraph (a) takes a positive line. The writer's judgement is clearly indicated; writer (a) outlines the way in which the question will be tackled, so the reader knows what to expect.

The author of paragraph (b) seems to be sitting on the fence. The first sentence is weak and the second sentence suggests that the writer is indecisive.

Conclusions

The conclusion needs to be strong too. This is after all what you leave the reader with. A good conclusion pulls the essay together. But it does this without falling into the trap of simply repeating what has been said, prefaced by some such phrase as 'Summing up, then...' or 'In conclusion...' or 'It can thus be seen that...'. A good conclusion will add something to the argument by such strategies as:

- placing the material in a different perspective;

- saving a good point to the end;

- indicating an area for further study.

2 Read the following conclusions (to the same essay title as that given in SAQ 1). Which seems to you the better conclusion, (a) or (b)? Why? (Cover my answer.)

a
> Thus it can be seen that society has in fact changed dramatically. This change has occurred in the areas of health, education, family life and transport — four key areas, each considered in the essay. The argument has been that the extent of change has been great, so much so that the phrase 'totally different' is justifiable.

b
> So in four key areas there has been dramatic change; the quotation is justified. But these changes have occurred not just as a result of new technology and new ways of organising institutions. Changes in attitudes, beliefs and values have been even more decisive and they have affected the details of daily life that tend to get ignored in discussions of social change.

It's difficult to judge without the whole essay. Also, I've made it complicated: neither of these is really bad, and neither is perfect. Conclusion (a) is conclusive and to the point but I prefer (b) myself because it is livelier. The writer of conclusion (b) has kept a good point to the end, giving an impression that there is more that could have been said. Writer (b) spends one sentence (the first) summing up and then introduces a new perspective. By contrast, conclusion (a) seems plodding. 'Thus it can be seen that...' is a rather weary phrase; this conclusion adds nothing new to what has gone before, though admittedly it is safe.

How long should introductions and conclusions be?

There's no easy answer to this. Much depends on the nature of the topic and on any length requirements in the question. If your essays are about 1,000 words long then you would need to allow approximately as follows:

Introduction 50–200 words
If the question is complex, and you need to spend time defining terms, then you might need up to 200 words; but this would be rare.

Main body 600–800 words
You should spend approximately 150–200 words on each of four main chunks.

Conclusion 50–200 words
If your introduction is long, then you probably won't also need to write a long conclusion.

Check your learning

1 Which of the following introductions would be best for an essay entitled 'The advantages and disadvantages of studying by means of a correspondence course'? Comment on each introduction.

a
> There are many different ways of studying. You can attend classes in a college or school. You can study from books, either bought from book shops or borrowed from a library.

b
> Correspondence study has a number of advantages and a number of disadvantages. First, though, I shall define what I take 'correspondence study' to mean.

c
> There are no advantages to studying by correspondence. It's just not possible to learn if you are not in contact with a tutor. And by contact I mean direct, face-to-face contact.

2 Which of the following statements is incorrect?

a A good conclusion places material in a new perspective.

b A good conclusion repeats what has already been said.

c A good conclusion adds something to the argument.

Read on only when you have answered the questions yourself.

Answers

1 Introduction (b) is certainly safest! Writer (b) is attending to the question and is aware of the need to define terms. Introduction (c) is much livelier but it jumps in too directly and is too loaded on one side. The question asks for both advantages and disadvantages. Introduction (a) is typical of an opening which doesn't answer the question and takes a long time to get going. The reader would be irritated because the writer shows no awareness of the question. What is said is obvious and uninteresting.

2 Statement (b) is incorrect. (Check back to the section on conclusions if you got this one wrong.)

GETTING YOUR ENGLISH RIGHT

What this unit is about

If you check back to Unit 2, you will see that we are now at the fourth stage of essay writing – editing. In Unit 6, we considered how to plan the coherence of the essay as a whole. In Unit 7, we looked at the translation of the plan into paragraphs. Now, we look at the third level of organisation in the essay: the individual sentence. (The diagram at the beginning of Unit 7 shows these three levels.)

By the time you have finished your work on this unit, you should be able to:

➜ work out a strategy for improving your English;

➜ punctuate with care.

How to write clearly

In Unit 1 I pointed out that to benefit from this book a reader should be able to write English with reasonable fluency. I am not able to cover all the skills of correct expression in this short unit. What I do hope to suggest is a strategy which we can all use to improve our writing.

This strategy has four elements:

1 draft and redraft;

2 build up your understanding of language and how it works;

3 work at punctuation;

4 work on improving your style.

1 Draft and redraft

Drafting is at the heart of this strategy. Sentences do not come out right first time; they need to be worked on.

1 In Unit 8 a section from one student's rough draft was presented as an example of drafting techniques. The student had marked some passages with an *E*, indicating problems in expression; these passages have been reproduced here. What do you think is wrong with each passage?

a

> Marriage in 1900 was sacred, you just didn't get divorced.

(continued overleaf)

> **b** *But there were some better things then about the family.*
>
> **c** *Family life has changed in lots of ways – more mobile, more flexible, each member tries to do more, women's role is more fluid, children are out more, other people take over family responsibilities (child minders, schools, playgroups).*

Passage a   This is very vaguely and casually expressed. The word 'you' is too colloquial for most essays.

Passage b   This idea could be more carefully expressed.

Passage c   This sentence is very long; there is too much information for a single sentence.

Some of the problems – especially the problem seen in passage (c) – would have been dealt with when the writer revised the paragraphing. The two levels – the paragraph and the sentence – are closely linked.

 Try rephrasing the three passages quoted in SAQ 1. Use your A4 sheet.

There are numerous ways to rephrase these sentences. Here are some possibilities:

a
> *In 1900 marriage was sacred; divorce was unthinkable.*

or

> *Divorce was often considered disgraceful in 1900, such was the sanctity of marriage.*

or

> *Divorce was a drastic step to take; in 1900 a marriage was sacred.*

(Note that there are always many different ways of saying the same thing. In drafting you can explore these different ways.)

b
> *But in some ways the family of 1900 was stronger than its counterpart today.*

or

> *There were, however, strengths in the 1900 family as well as weaknesses.*

or some alternative of your own.

c

> *Family life has changed in many ways. The family unit is more flexible and the woman's role in particular is now less rigidly defined. The family is more mobile; it may, for example, move house several times. Responsibilities for the children are shared by parents with other agencies in the wider society. These agencies include child minders, schools and playgroups. The result of all these changes is that the individual members of a family undertake more activities and commitments than their 1900 counterparts.*

These examples show the value of drafting. You don't think perfect thoughts and then write them down first time in perfect language. You think things out while writing them; to write is to learn (see Unit 2). The final stage is to make sure that your thoughts emerge in language that your reader will understand.

Two simple steps can help you to revise your drafts more effectively.

■ **Type or wordprocess your work**

It does help if you can see what you write in cold type. What you think looks fine in handwriting can look quite different in typeface. You can then see what you need to change.

■ **Read your work aloud**

Read it as if you were someone else looking at it. Ask a friend to read it. Note any awkward or unclear sentences and rewrite them.

2 Build up your understanding of language and how it works

Please note that this does not mean studying grammar or learning rules. Trying to learn rules (e.g. for spelling and punctuation) often only increases confusion. What you need is common sense. Most mistakes are the result of a lack of care or a lack of willingness (see Unit 1) or a failure to allow enough time for drafting. As I mentioned in an earlier unit, the best way to learn to write is to write; like any other skill you learn it by doing it. You also learn (again like any other skill) from comments on your performance, especially those made by your tutor. You gradually build up a realistic idea of where your strengths and weaknesses are, and of how you can improve. You'll return to this in Unit 12.

As well as writing try to read widely. Think about the ways in which other writers use words. Curiosity about words is a characteristic shown by most writers. Robert Louis Stevenson, for example, said:

> *I kept always two books in my pocket, one to read, one to write in – thus I lived with words...*

Having a general interest in language will lead, in time, to greater confidence in using it.

If you want to expand your vocabulary and improve your spelling, you might find *How To Use Your Dictionary,* another book in this series, helpful. See Appendix 4, 'Further reading', for more information on this.

3 Work at punctuation

English is governed by customs (or 'convention') rather than by rules. Punctuation is one of the conventions of expression and it often worries students. It helps, first, to get punctuation into perspective. Think of it as a way of making your reader's job easier. When we speak we 'punctuate' quite naturally; our voice indicates emphasis in the ways described in Unit 2. Marks like the comma and full stop have been devised to show pause and emphasis in the written language.

The full stop and comma are crucial. The full stop is most important of all. It separates one sentence or unit of thought from another. If you think of a full stop as marking off a whole unit, then a comma marks off one part of that unit from another part. Exclamation marks and question marks, both of which are rarely needed in essays, have exactly the same function as full stops.

The semicolon is less important but can be very useful. It is more emphatic than a comma but less so than a full stop.

The colon normally says 'stop; a list is coming', the dash says 'what follows is a comment on the side'. Neither of these is particularly important; the dash can be messy and a comma will usually serve instead. Brackets are used for asides but, again, you shouldn't need to use them often and their job can generally be done by commas.

A summary, then, of what you should learn about punctuation:

■ Full stops and commas are vital.

■ Semicolons are useful if you can master them.

■ Full stops mark off sentences.

■ Commas mark off fragments of sentences.

How can you learn to punctuate better? I suggest the following:

■ Examine the punctuation in the books you read. Start by looking at the punctuation marks I have used in this book; work out why I have used these marks and not others.

■ Read your work very carefully. Read it aloud, slowly, sentence by sentence. Ask yourself 'Where are the pauses? How long do I want my reader to pause here?'

■ Build up an awareness of your strengths and weaknesses in punctuation. Classify your errors, e.g:

    – not recognising a sentence (full stop);

    – not marking off fragments of a sentence (comma);

    – not using (or misusing) semicolons.

When your tutor indicates an error write out a corrected version of the sentence in which the error occurs.

Ask a friend to pick a passage from a book, newspaper or magazine and to copy it out removing all punctuation marks. You then punctuate it. You can compare your version with the original. (The aim is not to do it exactly as the original, your version may be better.)

If you want more help with punctuation, try *Mind The Stop*, a useful book by G V Carey. For information on this reference, see Appendix 4, 'Further reading'.

4 Work on improving your style

Style is a very large and much debated subject. What is 'good' style? What is 'bad' style? One intriguing (but not very helpful) definition is that good style is invisible, while bad style keeps getting in the way. Style is also a personal matter: inasmuch as it reflects the writer's own ideas and patterns of thought, it can't really be taught. But here are some general guidelines to help you improve your own writing style.

- Say one thing at a time; 'one idea, one sentence' is a useful reminder.
- Avoid long rambling sentences.
- Avoid jargon; use your own words.
- Avoid the pompous, the roundabout, the wordy and the colloquial.
- Use the active, not the passive (e.g. 'they thought' rather than 'it was thought').
- Use the positive rather than the negative.

There are numerous books on style. Three helpful ones are cited in Appendix 4, 'Further reading': *The Way To Write* by John Fairfax and John Moat; *How A Writer Works* by Roger Garrison; and *Report Writing* by Roger Lewis and John Inglis.

Check your learning

1 a What's wrong with the following sentence? (It is taken from a book review prepared by a student for an English exam.)

> This book leads us to imagine a world without machines — or at least a country and we are left to ask ourselves which one is the best — or is neither better than the other.

b Rephrase the sentence.

2 Which of these two approaches to the teaching of written expression best represents the view of the author of this book?

a Teaching students 'grammar' and then letting them express themselves through writing.

b Helping students use the drafting technique, to learn to write by writing.

3 What's wrong with the following extracts from the work of university students? Rewrite each sentence, correcting the errors.

a
> We see Claudius' conscience working on him, he sees it as a terrible thing to kill his own brother, but how else was he to obtain the crown, fulfill his ambition and marry the queen.

(by a student in an English literature course)

b
> Visions of a world run by computers with everyone leading a life of leasure.

(by a student in Electrical Engineering)

c
> The spelling has went through a limited amount of change.

(by a student in an English language course)

Read on only when you have answered the questions yourself. Use the A4 sheet.

Answers

1 a   The ideas are expressed in a loose and careless way. (Dashes often suggest that the writer is in a hurry.) More time should have been spent drafting. The writer has left the reader to complete the job for him.

     b   It is difficult to find an appropriate way to rephrase this sentence because the thought in the original seems so confused. But this is one possible way:

> *This book asks us to imagine a country without machines. It invites us to ask ourselves which is better – having machines or being without them. Or is there really no difference?*

2   I emphasise (b). If you got this wrong, re-read the section 'How to write clearly' in this unit.

3 a   There is a misspelling ('fulfill') and you could argue that there ought to be a question mark at the end. But the major problem (and a common fault in student writing) is that a comma is used where a full stop or semicolon is needed.

Suggested redraft:

> *We see Claudius' conscience working on him. He sees it as a terrible thing to kill his own brother; but how else was he to obtain the crown, fulfil his ambition and marry the queen?*

        Notice that I have also replaced the comma after 'brother' with a semicolon. A longer pause is required there than after 'crown' later. The balance of semicolon (after 'brother') and comma (after 'crown') gets the pauses right.

     b   'Leasure' is a misspelling of leisure. But the main problem is that this is not a complete sentence. It could be rewritten like this:

> *Many people have visions of a world run by computers with everyone leading a life of leisure.*

     c   It should read something like this:

> *The spelling has undergone a limited amount of change.*

(I'm grateful to Philip Hobsbaum, Reader in English at Glasgow University, for these examples. Any student who feels self-conscious about their writing can take comfort in noting that even university students of English make mistakes.)

PRESENTATION

What this unit is about

When you have revised your essay – checking for any problems in spelling, punctuation, style and expression – you are ready to copy it out and send it to your tutor. This short unit is a checklist of points you need to consider.

By the time you have finished your work on this unit, you should be able to:

➜ prepare a clear final copy of an essay, using an appropriate layout.

Before writing the final copy

Be sure to check your draft carefully before you make your final copy. Read each sentence again, with a careful eye for any spelling mistakes or punctuation errors that might have escaped your notice before. Be sure that there are no awkward or unclear sentences.

Check any quotations you have used. Make sure that they are accurate.

Quotations must be presented in a special way in essays, so that the reader knows precisely which words are yours and which belong to another author. You must put inverted commas around the words you have quoted, and give the source and the page number.

> Marriage in 1900 was taken very seriously. It was seen as a 'contract for life' (Stevens, p. 68).

> Marriage in 1900 was taken very seriously:
>
> 'In those days marriage was sacred. It was seen as a contract for life'
>
> (Stevens, p. 68).
>
> This attitude has now largely passed.

If you are quoting poetry, then either keep the lines in their original scheme, as in Example A (overleaf), or indicate line breaks by an oblique (/), as in Example B:

Example A

A group of poets called the Imagists, writing earlier this century, placed strong sharp, visual images at the centre of their poems:

'Their dresses were splashed on the green
Like big petals'

(Scannell, Picnic on the Lawn)

These lines create a powerful visual effect.

Example B

as above but

'Their dresses were splashed on the green/Like big petals'

If you are quoting from a play, then be sure to include the act, scene and line numbers. You will also usually need to give the edition of the play, for example (for Shakespeare) 'Arden' or 'Oxford'.

When you refer to another author's idea in the essay itself – even if you do not quote the author directly – you must identify the source of the idea:

Marriage then was taken very seriously, defined by some writers as a contract (Stevens).

You must list the sources of all your quotations in a booklist at the end of the essay, arranged alphabetically by the author's surname. This booklist should also include any materials that you consulted for your research and which have served as sources for the ideas in your essay. The author, title, publisher and date of publication of each source are included, for example:

Freeman, Richard and Meed, John 'How to Study Effectively',
CollinsEducational and the National Extension College, 1993.
Northedge, Andrew, 'The Good Study Guide', Open University Press, 1990.
Maddox, Harry, 'How to Study', Pan, 1988.
Rowntree, Derek, 'Learn How to Study', Macdonald, 1988.

Don't worry too much at this stage about the mechanics of identifying your sources. Some courses require detailed footnotes and elaborate bibliographies. Your tutor will show you the forms that are appropriate for the subjects you are studying. With a little practice, you'll find that this aspect of essay writing becomes second nature.

Writing the finished copy

You need to present the work as clearly and as attractively as possible for your reader. You have, after all, worked hard on your essay and you want to show it off to best advantage. Your final essay should, at the very least, be clear, tidy and legible. This is only courteous to the reader. Don't spend too long on the presentation, but it is important to observe certain aspects of layout:

- Leave a margin of about 4 cm (1/2 inches) on the left hand side of the page. This space is for your tutor's comments.

- Leave a space of about 8 cm (3 inches) at the bottom of the page, also for comments.

- If you type (and it does help!) then use double-spacing and type on one side of the paper only.

- If at all possible keep a carbon copy of your essay, in case the original gets lost.

- Write your essays on A4 paper (the standard size these days).

- Some essay questions include clear and specific advice on layout. They may ask you to tackle the question under certain headings (e.g. [I] A Survey of the Research, [II] The Problem Defined, [III] The Experiment... etc.). You should, of course, follow such instructions meticulously.

If you write your essays by hand

Handwritten essays are acceptable, but you must be sure that your handwriting is neat and clear. Use pen, not pencil, and write on lined paper. If you feel that your handwriting could be improved, try the following activity:

a   Give a specimen of your handwriting to a couple of friends. Ask them to underline any letters, or combinations of letters, which they find difficult to read.

b   Get your friends to tell you what it is about these underlined sections that causes difficulty, e.g. words crowded; words joined; loops from one line getting tangled up with those of lines above or below.

c   Analyse your problems in the light of (a) and (b) and try to put things right

This activity comes from *How To Study*, by Harry Maddox. For more information about this book see Appendix 4, 'Further reading'.

After writing the finished copy

Proofread your essay to make sure that there are no spelling or punctuation errors in your final copy. Mistakes nearly always seem to creep in, as authors of books know to their cost. One useful proofreading technique is to begin at the end of your essay and read it backwards (i.e. last sentence first). Starting at the end ensures that your attention is focused on individual words, rather than on the overall meaning of each paragraph.

Proofreading typeset copy

Occasionally, on really important occasions, your work may be printed. In this case, you will receive a 'proof copy' and you will be asked to note down any mistakes you see. There is a special printer's code of marks to show the various errors. Some of the marks are shown on the next page. To use them, circle or underline the letters or words you want to change, and put the relevant mark in the margin.

b/   cross out this letter and put b (or whatever it should be) instead

⊙/   put in a full stop that is missing

∧/   put in words or letters that are missing (write the missing words in the margin)

u.c./   make this letter a big one (upper case)

l.c./   make this letter a small one (lower case)

⌒/   join up this word that has fallen apart

#/   space out these words that have stuck together

ϑ/   rub this out.

The copy then goes back to the printer for corrections.

Check your learning

1 Name at least one matter to attend to:

    a   before writing the finished copy;

    b   while writing the finished copy;

    c   after writing the finished copy.

Read on only when you have answered the questions yourself. Use the A4 sheet.

Answers

1 Check back to the unit. Several matters are mentioned at (a) and (b); really only one (proofreading for mistakes) at (c).

UNIT 12

LEARNING FROM COMMENTS

What this unit is about

The job isn't over when you've sent the essay to your tutor. There's a great deal you can learn about essay writing from your tutor's comments.

By the time you have finished your work on this unit, you should be able to:

→ identify a range of different kinds of comment a tutor might make on an essay;

→ use tutors' comments to improve your work;

→ take advantage of the comments that friends make on your work.

Marks

Adult students, particularly, may have unhappy memories of the way their work was 'marked' at school – 0/10, a few ticks but many crosses, the occasional 'Satisfactory' or 'Poor'. Such students, returning to some form of study, are often very worried about getting their essays back from their tutor. They expect to be slapped down; they expect only their weaknesses to be pointed out.

It's not surprising that students have negative views like this; none of us likes criticism. But students should be able to establish a more collaborative relationship with their college tutor.

A good tutor will try to:

a   indicate your strengths as well as your weaknesses;

b   work out what the root causes of your weaknesses might be;

c   suggest ways that you can improve your work.

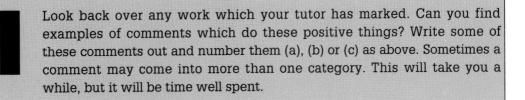

1   Look back over any work which your tutor has marked. Can you find examples of comments which do these positive things? Write some of these comments out and number them (a), (b) or (c) as above. Sometimes a comment may come into more than one category. This will take you a while, but it will be time well spent.

It pays to analyse your tutor's comments to the full. Comments generally fall into eight categories:

1   Overall comments: look first at what is said about the essay as a whole, either at the end or on a separate piece of paper. If a mark or grade has been awarded then you should find it justified here.

Then look at the detailed comments made on the essay itself (in the margins). These may include:

2   Comments on your ideas, i.e. on the content of the essay.

3   Comments on the structure of your essay (at the level of overall plan or paragraphing).

4   Comments on your expression (at the sentence level).

5   Comments suggesting new ideas or examples.

6   Corrections of fact.

7   Questions about your sources or about other conventions connected to your own subject.

8   In addition there may be comments (either in the essay or at the end)

- referring you to other parts of your course;

- relating the essay to others you have done;

- questioning you about how you carried out the essay (your way of working, how long it took, etc.).

Give each of the following comments one of the numbers 1–8. The numbers refer to the kinds of comments I have just listed. (Some may be given more than one number.) Comment (e) is done for you as an example.

a
> I give you a 7 for this — the quality of your argument is very high but one or two points about your expression let you down.

b
> Where did you get this quotation from?

c
> Does this sentence make sense?

d
> This is a much better essay than your previous one: did you find the topic easier?

e
> This treaty was concluded in 1816, not 1821.

f
> Check paragraphing — do these two link properly?

Comment (e) – 'This treaty was concluded in 1816, not 1821' – is a correction of fact. This is category 6 of tutor comments.

a 1. It's an overall comment, explaining the mark. You might also have said 2 or 4 – although this comment definitely seems to come from a comment at the end of an essay. Examples of 2 and 4 would probably be pointed out in the margins.

b 7

c 4

d This could be either 1 or 8

f 3.

3 Take each of the comments (a) to (f) in SAQ 2. Make a brief note in each case of what the student might usefully do, assuming he or she agrees with each comment. I've done the first one for you, as an example.

a *In drafting pay particular attention to expression OR*

Get a friend to read the next essay to see if they can find anything wrong.

You may have written something like the following:

b Record sources more carefully (Unit 5 and Unit 11).

c In drafting pay particular attention to expression **OR**

Ask a friend to read over the rough draft.

d Write back to the tutor in reply to this question.

e Take more care over recording details. Maybe there was carelessness at the stage of collecting material (Unit 5).

f Check paragraphing next time (along the lines suggested in Unit 7).

Carry out this activity for your own work; it will help you to diagnose which parts of this book you can usefully refer back to.

4 Check back over some of your own essays. Find examples of some of the kinds of comment just mentioned. Write out between five and ten of these, covering the range of comments possible. Are there any kinds of comments your tutor rarely or never seems to make? This may take up to an hour; again, though, it should pay off for you.

It's important to use every one of these comments to the full. If you agree with them, then try to put the advice into practice.

5 What have you learned from your tutor's comments?

If you disagree with your tutor's comments, or find you can't understand them, then you should raise the matter with your tutor, as this student does:

> *You say my points are muddled, but I spent a long time planning the essay. I can't really see any other way of organising them – can you help?*

Your tutor will welcome your responses to his or her comments: it shows you are attending to them. Much better to discuss a problem than to leave it unresolved.

 6 Have you found any of your tutor's comments hard to understand (or to read)? Have you disagreed with any of them? Give examples.

 7 Apart from submitting an essay, how often do you speak with, or write to, your tutor? What issues have you raised – your work in general, a particular point? A grade?

Here are three students writing about the ways in which they use their tutor's comments:

> As I am cut off from other students, I find the tutor comments give an additional 'slant' on points I might otherwise have missed.

> Where the comments have pointed to technical weaknesses in an essay, I have made efforts to correct this in the next one, e.g. too much description instead of analysis – poor structuring say, of any given essay — overuse of quotations as a substitute for analysis. Towards an examination, I read through the comments again to see if any old faults have crept back into my style.

> First of all I look for encouragement, this always gives me the boost to do better! I look for constructive criticism and keep this in mind to work from.

Using the comments of others

You'll remember that we suggested in Unit 10 that your friends or family could read your essays in draft and give you helpful comments. You could ask them:

- What did you enjoy in my essay?

- What did you find interesting?

- Did you understand it all? If not, which parts seemed hard or confused?

- Could you follow my argument throughout? Was it well planned and organised?

- Are the opening and ending effective?

- Did I support my ideas fully enough?

- What would you like to know more about?

All the comments you get on your work (from both friends and tutors) should help you to get better at the crucial skill of developing an awareness of where you are weak and where you are strong. As you develop this, so you will become increasingly confident and able to evaluate your own work.

If you want to read more about analysing essays, two books are particularly helpful: *How to Succeed in Exams and Assessments*, another book in this series and *Learning to Study*. See Appendix 4, 'Further reading', for more information on these books.

Conclusion

You have now worked through to the end of this book. Congratulations! You have considered and practised an approach to essay writing that involves four main stages:

■ pre-writing;

■ planning;

■ drafting;

■ editing.

(Check back to Unit 2 for an overview of these stages.)

You will probably have identified aspects of your work that could be improved. Use this book selectively as a guide to further work on these aspects. Further work is inevitable; no one is the perfect writer and we can all learn more. The more aware we are of this, the more we are likely to learn. Don't expect sudden and miraculous changes; learning of this kind takes time, practice and encouragement. Change is gradual.

Many students think that, somewhere, the recipe exists for writing perfect essays. But writing is a complex and personal matter, and the quality of what you write depends on a whole range of things – on your interest in the topic, on the time you have available, on your tutor – as well as on the more specific essay writing skills such as organising your thoughts clearly in writing. The four stages discussed in the book give you a framework to use when thinking about your practice.

Experienced writers set about writing in their own individual ways, though all do seem to go through certain stages and procedures. As a final note, I've included an extract from Roger Garrison's *How A Writer Works*, a very useful manual on the techniques of professional writers. This extract summarises the things that effective writers seem to have in common. You might find it worthwhile to read this over from time to time, as you develop *your own* way of writing.

■ They do not count on being 'inspired'. They write regularly, whether they feel like it or not. They force themselves to produce a specific amount of material even if much of it is junk. This is the toughest commitment.

■ They know that the act of writing generates ideas and information. They know that writing is discovery.

■ They do not usually write unless they face a deadline. But they make commitments, often self-imposed, that force them to write.

■ They make some kind of plan before they try a draft. This may be a list or a rough outline. Such a plan is flexible, and they can continue to add and adjust as they write.

■ They work in stages. Writers seldom plan to finish a piece of writing in a single session. They revise and rewrite, usually through several drafts.

■ They work slowly. If a first draft comes quickly, the rewriting may drag on. They persist, making changes as they go.

■ They continually go back to reread what they have written – to get the stimulus going again, and to remind themselves of the direction they are headed in.

■ They have writing blocks: times when they get stuck. They try free writing, or skip to another portion of a piece; or make further notes; or even copy what they have previously written. They look for *flow*.

- They may put off writing – any excuse: cleaning the house, or taking too many notes, or scribbling bits for another piece. But they recognise these digressions for what they are, and they are ruthless with such postponements.

- They often follow specific rituals: writing in the same place; using certain coloured paper for drafts; setting particular times for writing and so on. This kind of continuity is important.

- They accept the fact that writing is difficult and exhausting but they also know that having written (even a first draft) is satisfying.

Taken from *How A Writer Works*, Roger Garrison, Harper and Row 1981

Check your learning

1   What follows is a tutor's comment on an essay. What kind of comments are made? (Look back to the eight types of comment listed earlier on in this unit, to prompt your response.)

> Your understanding of the material is, again, very sound indeed. I thought that your own two arguments (in Part 2) hung together very well. I've concentrated on only very minor points but I assume that you'd like me to pick you up even on detail. Watch the occasional spelling. A useful book for you to buy on this would be 'How to use your dictionary' – from Collins/NEC. Basically, your spelling is fine but there are one or two words to note. The other thing is that you tend to use the comma rather too frequently. Can you see what I'm getting at and let me know if not?
>
> Very small points!

2   How many of the following are true?

a   Each writer has their own individual way of working.

b   There is a recipe for writing perfect essays.

c   All writers seem to go through more or less the same stages of composition.

Read on only when you have answered the questions yourself.

Answers

1   This is an overall evaluation which includes reference to ideas, structure and expression.

2   Statements (a) and (c) are true. (See the section headed *Conclusion* if you are unsure.)

APPENDIX 1

SETTING YOUR OWN ESSAY TITLE

Most courses require you to answer set questions. The teacher decides what you should focus on in a particular topic and how you should organise your thoughts on it (e.g. 'Explain...', 'Describe...', 'Compare and contrast...'). The teacher has already determined what kinds of response are appropriate for the question.

But you sometimes have to set your own title (even sometimes your own topic), especially in more advanced courses. This is more exciting but it can be daunting to many students. You have to make a series of choices. Let's suppose, for example, that you are preparing a paper on ageing and that you can deal with this in any way you like. You may decide to consider:

- the implications of greater life expectancy for the social services;

- the educational consequences (e.g. courses for the elderly);

- problems of health care for the aged;

- the psychological effects of ageing;

- the advantages of growing old (absence of job pressures, opportunity to travel);

- the way our society treats the elderly as compared with other societies or cultures.

Faced with such choices, how do you decide which direction to take? The first thing to say is that you should not decide too quickly. It's tempting to want to 'get on with it' and to start writing. But this can lead to frustration and wasted effort. You need first to explore. Brainstorming (Unit 4) is a good way to start. Write down what you know about the subject, what interests you, what you would like to know more about.

After you have this down on paper, ask yourself questions about what you have written. Are any patterns or directions apparent to you? Where do your thoughts seem to be leading you? Try to shape questions about what you have written, using the 'key verbs' listed and defined at the end of Unit 3 (analyse, describe, evaluate, etc.). These questions may well lead you to outside sources of information that can direct your thinking into useful channels. They can also help you to define a title for your essay.

What if you don't know enough about the subject to get very far by brainstorming? Background reading or assessing the available sources can be a useful way of getting started. Your local library can help here. Skim through books dealing with the topic; use tables of contents and indexes. At this stage, of course, you cannot be certain which of the articles and books you are sampling may eventually prove useful. Therefore, it is vital to list the sources you consult and briefly detail what they contain. This will save you much trouble later when you know what you are looking for.

As you discover what is available and what interests you, you should begin narrowing the topic to manageable dimensions. You can't adequately cover the whole of ageing (or of any other broad topic for that matter), so be selective. Just how much you narrow your topic depends on how long your essay has to be, on the time and energy you have to devote to your research and writing and on the resources available to you. You should settle upon a topic that you can master.

Once you have decided on your topic then take notes from those sources that are relevant to it. It may seem inefficient to have to return to the same sources you only skimmed before, but now your purpose is clear.

The advice given in this book can easily be adapted to meet the requirements of essays which you have to set for yourself. The disciplines of collecting information, organising it, paragraphing, drafting and editing apply in just the same way. The difference from pre-set essay titles is that you can delay decisions on the actual title until quite late on, until your interest becomes clear. Many writers do, in such circumstances, leave the precise formulation of the title until some drafting has been carried out.

Check your learning

1   What should you do first, if you have to set your own title?

2   The appendix suggests that you may need to use the same source on two quite different occasions and for two different purposes. Explain (briefly) why.

3   'The advice given in this book is relevant to essays you set yourself.' True or false?

Read on only when you have answered the questions yourself.

Answers

1   You may have written something like: 'Explore the topic' or 'Brainstorm' or 'Limit the options'.

2   You meet the source first while sampling or exploring. At this stage you may merely skim it and briefly note down what it contains. Then later, when you are clearer about what your essay will cover, you may need to read it closely, taking detailed notes.

3   True, though it may need a little adaptation on occasions. See the last paragraph of this appendix.

APPENDIX 2

ESSAYS IN EXAMINATIONS

Your approach to writing essays in an examination should be exactly the same as your approach to writing other essays, except that the whole process is speeded up and is far more concentrated. Be sure to keep the following points in mind:

■ Choose your questions carefully, going for ones you think you will do well and bearing in mind your own strengths and weaknesses.

■ Understand all instructions and act on them (answer the right number of questions; divide your time equally between them).

■ Allow a few minutes to collect material and to plan each answer, e.g.:

– underline key ideas;

– jot down questions, points, examples;

– arrange these in an appropriate order.

■ Write clearly (and quickly!) remembering that you will make a good impression if you show that you have looked closely at the question and are answering it. Never answer a question you wish had been set! (You will not have time in the examination to make a rough draft.)

■ Allow a few minutes at the end of the examination to check your work quickly for coherence at all levels: overall structure, paragraphing, sentences.

If you have worked hard on your course, and practised your essay writing then you will find that most of this will come as second nature.

Check your learning

1   Which of the following statements is bad advice?

a   You should choose carefully a topic which you know something about.

b   You should not worry too much about choosing which essay to do since they are usually all much the same as one another.

c   You should choose a topic which interests you, if you possibly can.

d   You should remember your strengths and weaknesses when choosing which essay to write in a course or in an exam.

Read on only when you have answered the questions yourself.

Answers

1   Statement (b) is unsound. Choice is very important, unless you really can answer all the questions equally well.

APPENDIX 3

AN ESSAY WRITER'S CHECKLIST

You might find it helpful to use this checklist for the next few essays you write.

Pre-writing

Unit 3   Have I identified any key verbs in the question?
Have I identified any key ideas in the question?

Unit 4   Have I brainstormed?
Have I probed?

Unit 5   Have I found suitable sources?
Have I used a variety of sources?
Have I made notes in my own words?
Have I noted all my sources?
Have I collected enough material?

Planning

Unit 6   Have I made a suitable plan?
Does my plan take account of any key verbs in the question?
Have I selected suitable material?
Is all my material relevant?

Unit 7   Does each paragraph have a clear, controlling idea?
Is the controlling idea adequately supported?
Have I signposted my reader?

Drafting

Unit 8   Have I taken my material through enough drafts?
Have I checked my drafts and redrafted so that:
- the ideas are in the right sequence?
- the structure of the essay is clear?

Unit 9   Have I written a sound introduction?
Have I written a sound conclusion?

Editing

Unit 10   Are my sentences clear?
Have I checked punctuation and spelling?
Is my style clear?
Have I read my essay aloud?

Unit 11   Is my essay within any stated word limit?
Is my essay clearly handwritten or typed?
Have I left space for my tutor's comments?
Have all sources and quotations been accurately recorded?

Learning from comments

Unit 12   Have I read carefully any comments on my returned essay?
Have I used these comments to the full?
Do I need to discuss these comments with my tutor (or anyone else)?

FURTHER READING

This is a list of books you may find helpful for further work. Some of them have already been mentioned; others will be new to you. You are not expected to buy or borrow from the library all or indeed any of these books. They are simply suggested as an optional extra if you wish to work further at particular aspects of essay writing.

Books on studying generally

Northedge, Andrew *The Good Study Guide*, Open University Press 1990

Freeman, Richard and Meed, John *How To Study Effectively*, Collins Educational and the National Extension College, 1993

Gibbs, Graham *Learning To Study*, National Extension College, 1980

Maddox, Harry *How To Study*, Pan, 1988

Rowntree, Derek *Learn How To Study*, Macdonald, 1988

Books on English expression

Carey, GV *Mind The Stop: a brief guide to punctuation*, Penguin, 1971

> Write to the National Extension College at 18 Brooklands Avenue, Cambridge, CB2 2HN for a list of current courses and publications on English expression.

Dictionaries and dictionary use

Collins Concise English Dictionary, Harper Collins, 1988

Concise Oxford Dictionary, Oxford University Press, 1990

Penguin Pocket English Dictionary (3rd edition), Penguin, 1990

Lewis, Roger and Pugmire, Martin *How To Use Your Dictionary*, Collins Educational and the National Extension College, 1993

Books on writing

Chaplen, Frank *Paragraph Writing*, Oxford University Press, 1970
(This book is now out of print, but you may be able to find it in a library)

Fairfax, John and Moat, John *The Way To Write*, Elm Tree Books, 1981
Excellent insights into the ways writers approach writing; very good on imaginative writing.

Garrison, Roger *How A Writer Works*, Harper and Row, 1981
(This book is now out of print, but you may be able to find it in a library)
Excellent guide to how professional writers work; good material on imaginative writing.

Lewis, Roger and Inglis, John *Clear Thinking*, Collins Educational and the National Extension College, 1993
Provides more practice in planning clear, logical essays.

Lewis, Roger and Inglis, John *Report Writing*, National Extension College, 1991

Henderson, Penny *How to Succeed in Exams and Assessments*, Collins Educational and the National Extension College, 1993
Good advice for students from GCSE upwards.

Theses and advanced projects

Berry, R *How To Write A Research Paper*, Pergamon Press, 1986

Parsons, CJ *Theses And Project Work*, Allen and Unwin, 1973
(This book is now out of print, but you may be able to find it in a library.)

For your notes

Other books in this series

Clear Thinking

John Inglis and Roger Lewis

An invaluable book for anyone who wants to organise and express their thoughts more effectively, or to analyse the arguments of others. Particularly useful for students preparing for assessment, whether verbally or in writing. Topics covered include: propositions and arguments; assertions; abuses of argument; using source material; applying clear thinking to poetry, prose, and art.

How to Succeed in Exams and Assessments

Penny Henderson

An interactive introduction to the key skills needed for assessment in the 1990s. Includes the latest information on assessment requirements for the new competence-based qualifications, as well as vital hints for tackling A level and GCSE exams. The book also shows how to cope with nerves and stress, and helps students develop their own personal strategy for success.

How to Study Effectively

Richard Freeman and John Meed

Enables students to identify their own aims and needs, and to prepare an action plan for effective study. All the essential skills of reading, writing and assessment are fully covered in a practical and reassuring way. Topics include: analysing your learning style; identifying learning techniques; effective reading; note-making; writing; assessment; using additional resources.

How to Use Your Dictionary

Roger Lewis and Martin Pugmire

Shows how dictionaries can be used to assist at many stages of study, from clarifying meanings and spellings to finding out about pronunciation and the origins of words. Includes numerous examples from a wide range of dictionaries. Topics include: using a standard dictionary; finding meanings; finding spellings; pronunciation; checking the history of a word.

Acknowledgements

Many people have helped in the generation of this book. I should particularly like to thank Richard Baker and Janet Bollen for their friendship and practical support over many years, Doug Spencer for his stimulating ideas on how people learn, and all the students and tutors who commented on the various drafts and earlier versions of this book.